A Short Guide to Writing about History

D0126412

THE SHORT GUIDE SERIES
Under the Editorship of
Sylvan Barnet
Marcia Stubbs

A Short Guide to Writing about Art by Sylvan Barnet

A Short Guide to Writing about Biology by Jan A. Pechenik

A Short Guide to Writing about Chemistry by Herbert Beall and John Trimbur

A Short Guide to Writing about Film by Timothy Corrigan

A Short Guide to Writing about History by Richard Marius

A Short Guide to Writing about Literature by Sylvan Barnet

A Short Guide to Writing about Science by David Porush

A Short Guide to Writing about Social Sciences by Lee J. Cuba

A Short Guide to Writing about History

Third Edition

RICHARD MARIUS
Harvard University

An Imprint of Addison Wesley Longman, Inc.

New York • Reading, Massachusetts • Menlo Park, California • Harlow, England
Don Mills, Ontario • Sydney • Mexico City • Madrid • Amsterdam

Editor in Chief: Patricia Rossi
Associate Editor: Lynn M. Huddon
Marketing Manager: Ann Stypuloski
Project Manager: Donna DeBenedictis
Design Manager: John Callahan
Text Design Adaptation: Sarah Johnson
Cover Designer: John Callahan
Cover Photo: Planet Art
Prepress Services Supervisor: Valerie Vargas
Electronic Production Specialist: Sarah Johnson
Senior Print Buyer: Hugh Crawford
Electronic Page Makeup: ComCom, a RR Donnelley & Sons Company
Printer and Binder: RR Donnelley & Sons Company
Cover Printer: The Lehigh Press, Inc.

For permission to use copyrighted material, grateful acknowledgment is made to the copyright holders on p. 185, which is hereby made part of this copyright page.

Library of Congress Cataloging-in-Publication Data
Marius, Richard.
    A short guide to writing about history / Richard Marius.—3rd ed.
        p.   cm.—(The short guide series)
    Includes index.
    ISBN 0-321-02387-0 (pbk.)
    1. Historiography. 2. History—Methodology. 3. History—Research.
4. Academic Writing. I. Title.
D13.M294   1999   98-20852
907'.2—dc21   CIP

Copyright © 1999 by Richard Marius

ISBN 0-321-02387-0

Please visit our website at http://longman.awl.com

12345678910—DOC—01009998

For my sons Richard,
Fred, and John.
For the miles we have
biked together
following history
under the soft skies of France.

Contents

Preface

This little book arose out of my experience of teaching European history for sixteen years—first at Gettysburg College and then at my alma mater, the University of Tennessee, Knoxville—and then out of the sixteen years I spent directing the Expository Writing Program at Harvard, where I regularly taught a course called "Writing about History."

Most students came into my courses believing that history was hardly more than a collection of names and dates to be memorized and repeated on examinations. They thought they could go to the library, look up several articles in encyclopedias, and write a paper to show how much they knew about a subject. They did not imagine that they could think for themselves about the facts. Sometimes they believed that "thinking" was to express vehement opinions, often about the supposed morality or immorality of the past they read and wrote about. Far too often they tried to write as though they were accomplished historians who had solved all the problems about some broad historical subject and could only scorn those who disagreed with them.

It was my job to teach them that history becomes most exciting when we study a collection of primary sources—the basic stuff from which history is made—to make sense of these sources and tell a story about them. Primary sources are by definition the sources closest to the events and people whose stories we seek to tell. They may be letters, diaries, and books published by participants in events. Woodrow Wilson, Thomas More, Martin Luther King, Jr., Virginia Woolf, Eleanor Roosevelt, and Toni Morrison all wrote extensively or spoke so that their words were recorded by others. These written materials are primary sources for their lives. Or primary sources may be the earliest reports of those who knew or claimed to know figures in the past whom we study in the present.

Historians and others have written about these primary sources. They have produced secondary sources—narratives, interpretations, and descriptions—to tell us what they think the primary sources mean. These secondary sources, as we call them, embody hard work and careful thought—and often disagree with one another. No one serious about the study of history can neglect this treasury of research and thought, and students should demonstrate in the papers they write in college that they are familiar with what other people have written about a topic. The best history papers show a balance between primary and secondary sources.

The best reasons for studying history are the same as those for studying all the liberal arts: historical study satisfies curiosity, and it enriches our minds. The most interesting human beings are those with curiosity. They ask questions. How did things get to be the way they are? Why have some names come down to us glittering with fame or stained with infamy? Why is this monument here? Why was this painting a scandal when it was first shown to the public? How did this book cause a revolution? Who built this amazing bridge?

History also provides us with the pleasure of vicarious experience—living in our imaginations lives others have lived in the past. It opens windows into the variety of human experience and reveals human nature, not in some abstract philosophical way but in the concrete actuality of what real human beings thought and did. History tells us how diverse human beings and their societies can be. If we study it attentively, it should make us more tolerant of people unlike ourselves because history reveals such an immense variety of successful human experiences.

The study of history has expanded in recent years. Only a generation or two ago in the United States, historians thought that the only history worth attention consisted of war and politics and that the only historical figures worth studying were great men, especially great men in Western Europe and the United States. Now historians study the history of women, the history of minorities in various countries including our own, the history of popular culture, the history of sexual practices, the history of science, military history, and heaven knows what else.

Sometimes this emphasis on social history can seem trivial, especially when it is driven by one-sided agendas. But it can also be fascinating and enlightening. In a recent article called "Gradually Entering the Realm of Delight: Food and Drink in Early Medieval China,"[1] Professor David R. Knechtges of the University of Washington considered not only what the Chinese ate more than a thousand years ago but what they drank, including forty kinds of alcoholic beverages. He showed that for the Chinese of that time, eating was a "source of pleasure that can be spiritually uplifting," and that the Chinese saw "eating and drinking almost as a form of art." His article reveals communal rituals in a society different from our

---

[1]*Journal of the American Oriental Society* (April–June 1997): 229–239.

own, where our fast-food habit allows us little opportunity for the social bonding that a leisurely, ritualistic meal helps seal. It helped me understand a little better why I was once served a thirteen-course meal after I had lectured in Taipei.

When history is written well about any topic, an interested audience waits to read it. Perhaps it is a small audience, but it is out there. In a striking fashion, Professor Knechtges's article also conveyed one of the benefits of studying the history of cultures different from our own: the study of other cultures enables us to see our own way of doing things— such as eating—from a different angle so that we don't fall into the error of imagining that our way is the only good way. It also makes an essential point that every budding historian should know: everything has a history. Nothing is too ordinary for the historian's scrutiny, and if we have sources and if we give our minds liberty, we can think and write about the history of almost anything.

Teaching people to write about history has been for me a means of showing students of all ages that they have worthwhile thoughts and can use them to write interesting and original essays on many subjects. As users of this book will, I hope, discover, the study of history involves a special kind of thinking, closely related to the way we solve puzzles and try to guess who the murderer is in a good mystery. Historical thinking is indeed a kind of game, and it has a deeply serious side—but it is also a lot of fun!

I hope the third edition of *A Short Guide to Writing about History* will continue to help students think about history, see its puzzles and its pleasures, and gain the confidence that good writing about anything requires. You must approach the task with the trust that you have the tools to do the job, and I hope you will find them in this little book.

SOME NOTES ON THE THIRD EDITION

Users of the second edition will find several changes in the third.

- Since 1994 when I completed my work on the second edition, the Internet and the World Wide Web have become facts of life for tens of thousands of college students. Electronic communication offers possibilities for research unimaginable only a few years ago. I have added sections on how to use and document sources taken from the Internet as well as several addresses of reliable Internet sites where valuable material for history students may be found. You will also find here a discussion of materials to be found on CD-ROM.

- Since many Canadian colleges and universities use this book, I have added several examples from Canadian history as well as new examples from U.S. and world history. I have sought to make the book more useful for courses across the discipline.
- This edition, like the last, includes more women historians than the previous one, and I have added examples from cultural, social, and women's history.
- Contemporary sources, including some from the Internet, have been added to the sample term paper in Chapter 5.
- I have placed the guidelines for writing book reviews into Appendix A.

A reward for writing a book is to hear from those who read and use it. Please write me with your thoughts about anything in *A Short Guide to Writing about History*. You can mail letters to me at the Department of English, the Barker Center, Harvard University, Cambridge, MA 02138. Or you may reach me on e-mail (rmarius@fas.harvard.edu). I shall always respond.

Acknowledgments

A number of historians at various colleges and universities in the United States and Canada offered priceless advice as I prepared the manuscript for the third edition. I worked with a pile of suggestions by my keyboard, consulting reviewer's remarks for almost every page. I am more grateful than words can express to Donald Bailey, University of Winnipeg; Nancy Gabin, Purdue University; Edward R. Geehan, United States Military Academy, West Point; Thomas C. Mackey, University of Louisville; Thomas C. Owen, Louisiana State University; Timothy J. Shannon, Gettysburg College; Philip Soergel, Arizona State University; Mark Wasserman, Rutgers University; Barbara Welter, Hunter College, CUNY; and Michael Winship, University of Georgia.

Lynn M. Huddon has been a devoted and remarkable editor. Unlike many textbook editors, she has taken an active and continual interest in the details of the book. Her measured and thoughtful suggestions have been cogent and wise, her cheerful patience with a somewhat temperamental writer amazing, and her insistence on deadlines sometimes like an alarm bell in the night telling me to get on with it. And so I did. I have worked with many editors; she is one of the best.

I live and move and have my being in a circle of friends without whom nothing would be worthwhile. As I have done so many times in the past, I offer heartfelt thanks to a life that has brought me many friends, including my brother John, and my wife of almost thirty years, Lanier Smythe.

The book is again dedicated with love to my three sons, Richard, Fred, and John.

RICHARD MARIUS

A Short Guide to Writing about History

Introduction

Students struggling over an essay in history have often told me that they know the subject but cannot write about it. They usually mean that they have a jumble of facts in their heads but cannot tell a story about them.

Their complaint represents a discovery: History is a special kind of thinking. It involves telling a story, and while facts are essential in telling a story, they are not enough. You can have a big, bad wolf, a little girl named Red Riding Hood, an old grandmother, a basket of cakes, and a dark woods without having a story. You can even know the date of the wolf's birth, the color of Red Riding Hood's hair, and the mailing address of the grandmother as well as her Social Security number, and still not have a story.

Stories have tension, presented usually right at the beginning. At the start we know that something will happen. People and forces contend with each other. Readers see tension, struggle, and the possibility that something is out of balance, and they read on to see how it all comes out. In writing an essay about history, you tell the story of your thinking about a topic wherein forces are opposed to each other with the outcome in doubt. You formulate a thesis to say that things happened this way and not another and that the reason they happened this way was because of this, this, and this. You allow for the possibility that if this or this or this did not happen, things could have turned out entirely differently.

Historians study sources that tell them about the past, and they write because they see something that needs to be explained. Like journalists, they ask who, what, where, when, and why. What happened? Who was responsible? Where did this event happen? When or in what order did things happen? Why did they happen? What have other historians said about the event? What mistakes did they make that I can now correct? The historian is a curious and relentless questioner.

Historians are like most of the rest of us. They want to know what events mean, why they were important to what came afterwards, why we still talk about them. When the people of Israel crossed the Jordan River into Palestine or "Canaan" after their Exodus from Egypt and their wandering in the desert, their leader Joshua commanded them to take twelve heavy stones from the river and set them in a pile on the western bank. He said that in years to come when children asked their parents, "What do you mean by these stones?" the parents would tell the story of how Israel crossed the Jordan with God's help. The stones were a memorial; that is, they made generations of Israelites remember. They made children ask questions that adults could answer.

Our public monuments do the same. A child standing below the Capitol of the United States, the great sculptured likeness of Ulysses S. Grant astride his horse, Grant looking South across the Washington Mall under the brim of his hat, will ask his or her parents, "Who is that?" And the parents can say, "This is the man who saved the Union, and made us a nation."

Questions rise from our monuments, our habits, our documents, our broader experience in the world. All historical writing begins as an effort to answer questions about origins, happenings, and consequences. We find a puzzle and try to solve it. When you write a paper for a history course, you must do the same—find a problem that stirs your curiosity and try to solve it. If you don't have a problem, you don't have a paper.

Here are the first two paragraphs of an article in *The American Historical Review (AHR)*, the leading journal for historians in the United States:

> In France during the 1920s, fashion was a highly charged issue. In 1925, an article in a journal called *L'oeuvre* ["The Work"] described how the fashion of short hair had completely overturned life in a small French village. After the first woman in the village cut her hair, accompanied by "tears and grinding of teeth" on the part of her family, the fashion had quickly become "epidemic: from house to house, it took its victims." A gardener swore he would lock up his daughter until her hair grew back; a husband believed that his wife had dishonored him. A scandalized priest decided to preach a sermon about it, but "unfortunately he had chosen the wrong day, since it was the feast of Jeanne d'Arc." As he began to condemn bobbed hair as indecent and unchristian, "the most impudent young ladies of the parish pointed insolently at the statue of the liberator." By claiming the bobbed-cut Joan of Arc as their mascot, these young women grounded their quest for "liberation" in the rich, tangled mainstream of French history. They appealed to the ambivalent yet strongly traditional image of *Jeanne la pucelle* (Joan the Virgin), at once patriotic, fervently Christian, and sexually ambiguous.
>
> The fashion among young women for short, bobbed hair created enormous tensions within the French family. Throughout the decade,

newspapers recorded lurid tales, including one husband in the provinces who sequestered his wife for bobbing her hair and another father who reportedly killed his daughter for the same reason. A father in Dijon sought legal action against a hairdresser in 1925 for cutting the hair of his daughter without his authority. "At present, the question of short hair is dividing families," argued Antoine, one of the hairdressers who pioneered the bobbed cut. "The result," according to journalist Paul Reboux, "was that during family meals, nothing is heard except the clicking of the forks on the porcelain." One working-class woman, who was in her twenties during the era, remembered that her mother-in-law did not talk to her sister-in-law Simone for almost a year after the latter bobbed her hair. René Rambaud, another hairdresser who helped to popularize the cut, recalled the story of a newly married woman who cut her hair, believing that she had the right to do so without consulting her parents. Her mother and father in turn accused her husband and his parents of the monstrous crime, leading to a rift so severe that the two families did not reconcile for twenty years.[1]

We read these few anecdotes and ask ourselves, "What was all the fuss about?" We expect answers, and Professor Mary Louise Roberts gives them to us. In her last past paragraph she sums up her conclusions:

> For historians trying to understand socio-cultural changes during the period of World War I, the controversy surrounding postwar fashion is a rich source for exploration. The ways in which French observers read the text of fashion can tell us much about what preoccupied and worried them during this time of transition. Many of the French, such as fashion's critics, yearned for a more traditional and stable French society, symbolized by the domestic hearth. They expressed anxiety that change would usher in a colder, more impersonal world. Others, namely the supporters of fashion, welcomed change as a dismissal of pre-war social constraints. Fashion was not "politics" as we are used to conceiving of it, but the debates over its meaning in postwar France were profoundly political. The fashions of the modern woman became central to the cultural mythology of the era, instilling at once envy, admiration, frustration, and horror, because they provided both a visual language for upheaval and changed and figured in a political struggle for the redefinition of female identity.[2]

[1]Mary Louise Roberts, "Samson and Delilah Revisited: The Politics of Women's Fashion in 1920s France," *The American Historical Review* (June 1993): 657–658. I have left out Professor Roberts's extensive footnotes for these paragraphs.

[2]Roberts, 684.

Professor Roberts, stirred by curiosity, sought the answer to a question: Why did the French after World War I make so much of the decision of some French women to cut their hair short? Today we may find it puzzling that anyone could care how women cut their hair. That puzzle interested Professor Roberts, and she wrote an essay to solve it.

Solving the puzzles of history involves science and art. Science is a synonym for knowledge. But knowledge of what? History includes data—evidence, the names of people and places, when things happened, where they happened, bits of information gathered from many sources. It also includes interpretations of historians and others in the past who have written on the topic that the writer decides to treat in an essay. The art of history lies in combining fact and interpretation to tell a story about the past. Professor Roberts did that in her article. She had data—the reports of the controversy stirred up in France when women cut their hair short after World War I. Her essay interprets what the data mean.

As time passes, legends and outright lies creep into history. Historians try to distinguish between the true and the false. In the sixteenth century some English writers called history "authentic stories" to distinguish it from fantastic tales about the past. Historians in the Renaissance set about examining sources, making judgments about what could be believed and what not. They searched for old documents, studied them to see if they were authentic, weeded out forgeries, and compared copies to find errors scribes had made in transmitting texts. They also compared different stories told about the same events. These historians tried to tell the truth—as do historians today.

But in the study of history, "truth" is complicated, contradictory, and usually obscure. History does not repeat itself. Every historical event happens one time and becomes separated from the present by the steady accumulation of other events happening day by day. We cannot put the assassination of President John F. Kennedy into a laboratory and make it happen again and again as we might conduct an experiment in chemistry, measuring and calculating to see precisely the relations of cause and effect. The event happened once—on Friday, November 22, 1963—and it will never happen again. To know that event we depend on the memories of those who were there, and, as they die off, the records they left us of Kennedy's death. These records may include sound and video recordings that make his murder more vivid than books and articles can do. But they are all records, subject to many interpretations and subject also to the tricks memory plays even on eyewitnesses. We can never relive the event exactly as it happened.

All historians confront an essential problem: The past is dissolving under our feet at every moment. The Romans had a proverb: *Tempus edax rerum*, "Time the devourer of things." Time destroys. The evidence for past events is always incomplete and fragmentary, like a jigsaw puzzle washed out of a shipwreck and cast upon a rocky beach by the waves. Many pieces are lost. Those that remain are often faded and warped. Historians fit the pieces together as carefully as possible but holes remain in the picture they try to reconstruct. They do their best to fill in the holes with inferences that seem plausible and that fit the available facts. What emerges may closely resemble what happened, but we can never be sure that what we know as history is exactly right. Our knowledge of history is always in flux, and historians are always in dialogue, not only with the primary sources of the events they write about but also with other historians of those events. To write history is to be engaged in endless argument.

WRITING HISTORY AS A WAY OF THINKING

History and writing are inseparable. We cannot know history well unless we write about it. Writing allows us to arrange events and our thoughts, study our work, weed out contradictions, get names and places right, and question interpretations—our own and those of other historians. In writing we work out the chronological order of events—not a simple task but one indispensable to the historian's craft.

Fluent talkers can touch on first one idea and then another, sometimes using body language to stress a point. They can overwhelm opposition by charisma or by shouting when their argument is weak. Writers perform a more daring act. They must develop an idea with logic and clarity, knowing that a reader can study their words again and again and discover whether the words add up to a plausible argument, given the evidence available. If writers are illogical, unfair, untruthful, confused, or foolish, their words lie on the page to be attacked by anyone with the care and interest to look. Good talkers can contradict themselves, waffle, and weasel, and on being called to task, can claim that their hearers misunderstood them, or they can say, "I didn't say that at all." Because our short-term memory is fallible, we may think we have indeed misunderstood. Because we are also usually polite, we may allow sloppy talkers to escape their confused expression by their dexterity in shifting words. Writers enjoy no such emergency exit. What they have written they have written, and it is on the page for all to see again and again. Writers must strive to be clear, logical, and fair, or they will be found out.

Good writing goes hand in hand with a sense of human possibility and limitation. No wonder that in some societies, such as ancient Israel, historians were priestly figures. They wrote in the light of their beliefs about the relation of God to humankind and therefore with an idea of human nature and the purpose of life. Our beliefs about what is possible for human beings will control our beliefs about what might have happened in the past. Can men and women be heroic? Are human beings always selfish, or can we be truly generous? Does human history move in response to leaders or in spite of them? Or are leaders thrust up by the society that in fact leads them? Are our strongest motivations for power, for wealth, for sex, or for community? Are we naturally aggressive, or do we prefer peace?

A student of mine once wrote that in 1215 King John of England "decided" to give the English people Magna Carta and guarantee them certain liberties. He made it sound as if King John had been struck one day with a benevolent impulse and decided on his own to give his people a gift. But in history, those with power have usually given it up or allowed it to be reduced only when they have been forced to do so. The real story of Magna Carta is not King John's benevolence but the forces that made him issue the document. In this light, the story of Magna Carta becomes in part a consideration of how human nature operates.

As important as any other question about human nature is this: Do we have any freedom of choice? Is history a series of important decisions that could have gone either way? Or is it a masquerade, a perpetual series of predestined events that no human will can control? Did Robert E. Lee have to fight the battle of Gettysburg as he did, or did he have a choice? Did President Harry S. Truman have a choice when he decided to drop the atom bombs on Japan to end World War II in 1945? Was the bomb necessary to end the war and to prevent an invasion of Japan in which millions of lives would have been lost? Or was he driven by the desire for revenge against Japan and the wish to make a demonstration of power against the Soviet Union after Japan was already effectively beaten? Or are all these explanations at least partly true?

Historians usually write as if people had the power to choose in the past. The tension between what historical figures did and what they might have done gives history part of its excitement. Herbert Butterfield, a philosopher of history, wrote, "History deals with the drama of human life as the affair of individual personalities, possessing self-consciousness, intellect, and freedom."[3] Tolstoy, by contrast, in his novel *War and Peace* wrestled with the idea of freedom, observing that "to conceive a man perfectly free, not subject to the law of necessity, we must conceive of a man *outside of space, outside of time, and free from all dependence on cause.*"[4] He wrestled with the problem of just how much freedom we have and what part of life is constrained by necessity. He concluded that leaders only *seem* to lead—that in fact they emerge out of the collective development of a power inherent in the masses of people. In writing about the past, historians may not say explicitly that their answers depend on their view of human nature or human freedom. Yet their answers depend on assumptions, sometimes unexpressed, about what is possible or probable in human nature and what is not.

Our times and our thoughts are shaped by the past. That shaping is one reason we study history. How we think, how we react to events in daily life, the vocabulary we use in speaking of the past—all are legacies. To study the past helps us understand better how we came to be who we are, helping us decide what to retain from the past and what to reject. By showing us that our lives are historically conditioned, we discover freedom, for we know that what *is* does not have to be this way.

Every part of the past has a unique quality. Every event we study in history existed in its own network of cause and effect, its own set of relations between people and events, its own modes of thought, usually taken for granted by the societies themselves, often assumed to be a divine ordination that could not be changed. A thunderstorm roars over the Kansas prairie today, and the television news meteorologist in his bright suit and hair spray explains with his million-dollar grin that the storm is the result of a collision between a cold front and a warm front. In ancient Mesopotamia, the Babylonians heard in the thunder the voice of their god Marduk and thought that he was hurling lightning bolts into the earth. In these and countless other ways, spontaneous responses to many experiences in the past were different from our own. Part of our task is to think our way into the minds of the people who lived in earlier times so we can think about experience as they did. Yet we can never fully abandon our own perceptions; we cannot recover the past exactly as people then thought of life and the world.

[3]Herbert Butterfield, *Christianity and History* (New York: Scribner's, 1950), 26.
[4]Leo Tolstoy, *War and Peace*, trans. Constance Garnett (New York: Modern Library, n.d.), 1131.

Sometimes historians try to distinguish between the unique qualities in events and the qualities that seem to repeat themselves. What qualities help some large states endure? What qualities doom others to fall? The earliest great empires in Western civilization were made possible when people learned to ride horses shortly after 2000 B.C. Armies on horseback could pass swiftly from place to place, appearing suddenly, striking terror in soldiers inexperienced with the noise and speed of such mighty animals. These empires rose swiftly and then swiftly collapsed. But centuries afterward the Roman Empire rose and endured for centuries. What circumstances made these early empires rise and fall with such bewildering speed? How was Rome different? Would our study of Assyria and Babylon illuminate in any way our understanding of the sudden and unexpected collapse of the Soviet Union? The questions are fascinating, but the answers are uncertain. One historian may see a pattern of repetition; another may see in the same events circumstances unique to a specific time and place.

Some Greek and Roman historians believed that history involved cycles of repetition and that to know the past allowed us to predict the future. Few modern historians would make such claims. Some broad patterns repeat themselves. Empires, countries, and cultures rise and fall. Protests against a dominant culture often show up in how people—especially young people—dress and wear their hair. To some scholars, these repetitions make it seem that all history is locked into invariable cycles. History becomes a treadmill on which human beings toil endlessly without getting anywhere.

Many nineteenth-century historians believed that history was the story of inevitable progress—culminating in the triumph of the white races because of their supposed superiority over people of color throughout the world. If today is good, tomorrow will be better. Other historians have seen history moving according to God's will. When people do good, they thrive; when they violate the laws of God, they decline and suffer.

But on close investigation, the swirls and waves of the historical process don't appear to move in predictable patterns. Those who assume that learning about the past will allow them to avoid mistakes in the future underestimate the continuous flow of the new into human events. New inventions or new ways of thinking or new combinations can upset all predictions. In 1914 both the French and the German generals in charge of planning for a war between their two countries expected the coming conflict to resemble the war between Germany and France in 1870–1871. In that earlier war, the Germans moved swiftly by railroad and on horseback, outmaneuvered the French, and determined the outcome of the war within three months. It was a war of motion—dramatic, soon over, without much damage to either side to property or human life.

The generals on both sides in 1914 expected another short war, not realizing the power of a new weapon, the machine gun, which slaughtered advancing soldiers in unimaginable numbers, creating a daily massacre that turned the conflict into a four-year standoff in opposing lines of trenches running from the Swiss border to the English Channel. In this long, hard war, millions died, and the north of France was devastated.

In 1940 the French, learning from the fatal experience of World War I, built a series of concrete forts across northern France called the Maginot Line, anticipating another war in which armies would face each other until one dropped from exhaustion. The Maginot Line was to be a sort of warm, dry, and safe trench made of reinforced concrete. The French planned without considering the new technology of that era—airplanes and swift armored tanks used by the Germans to defeat the French in forty days of *Blitzkrieg* (lightning war).

At the very least, experiences such as these teach us to be cautious in suggesting what history can tell us of both present and future. For one thing, we no longer predict inevitable progress in human affairs. We don't burn witches anymore. But we still manage to slaughter millions of our fellow human beings for reasons that seem as irrational as accusations of witchcraft.

So our contemporary experience confirms our caution in how we interpret history. We can know history well and still be startled by events. In recent decades, thousands of historians young and old studied the history of the Soviet Union. The Central Intelligence Agency employed historians to help our government understand how to deal with the Soviet Union and predict what it might do. Yet not one of these scholars predicted anything like the sudden collapse and breakup of the great Soviet empire in 1989 and 1990.

And what of the place of leaders in history? The current mood in historical studies is to be skeptical about how much individual leaders may accomplish on their own. We seem to be closer to Tolstoy than to Butterfield. Historians know that any particular event in history is brought into being by a complex of contributing forces—some visible and some difficult to identify. What caused the American Revolution? The popular answer was oppression of American colonies by Britain, the mother country, and most of us can probably recite events that goaded the colonies to revolt—the Stamp Act, the Boston Massacre, the tax on tea and the consequent Boston Tea Party, and finally the skirmishes at Lexington and Concord on April 19, 1775, when someone fired "the shot heard 'round the world." Leaders such as John Hancock, Sam Adams, John Adams, James Otis, and others in Massachusetts were said to be leaders of an almost unanimous populace. That, at least, was the history of the American Revolution as many of us learned it in grade school and in the popular mythology spread by Fourth of July oratory.

On examination, British "oppression" seems much less severe than once commonly supposed, American support for the Revolution far less than unanimous, and leadership of the patriot forces much more ambiguous. Historians now search for deeper causes that provoked a substantial number of Americans to want their independence from Great Britain enough to fight for it. Yes, Americans had great orators such as Sam Adams and Patrick Henry. But orators are nothing unless they have an audience, and our experience in the present shows us that orators don't change people's minds so much as they provide words for feelings that people already have. What groups were dissatisfied and willing to listen to the patriot orators? Why? What groups were content under British rule and why? What role did American women and the American clergy play? To what degree was the American Revolution a class struggle within colonial American society? How much of the Revolution's success came because the British were more concerned with their war with France than with their rebellious colonies? Here is a puzzle where there are many more pieces than "leaders" and "followers." Here are two complex populations, Americans and British, in continual flux with not only different motivations but different degrees of intensity, and different resources. Somehow out of this confused mix, the American Revolution happened. Historians must acknowledge that the relations between causes and effects are more complicated than any simple explanations can allow.

Historians nowadays don't reject the role of the individual altogether. Biography remains the form of history most read by the general public, and biographies by their nature emphasize the individual. Still, a mood among historians sees the individual working under more complicated restraints, with more ambiguity and with both less success and less abject failure than biographers once admitted. We have moved away from the Renaissance view of history that held it to be a collection of moral examples. From the Renaissance until modern times, biographers attempted to provide heroes to be imitated or villains whose examples were to be shunned. Now the emphasis is less judgmental, more dispassionate, more balanced—although on occasion this or that historian can still erupt in moral indignation at past wrongs.

Historians now study sources and deal with issues that once drew little attention at all. For centuries the writing of history was almost entirely about what men did. If women entered the story, it was because they did things male historians generally expected men to do. They ruled countries as did Queen Elizabeth I of England; they refined radium, as Marie Curie did in France; they wrote novels, as many women have done for several centuries—some like George Eliot in England and George Sand in France using male pseudonyms to gain acceptance. Now historians are turning to many other areas of historical interest. A random glance through recent issues of the *AHR* will show titles such as Elizabeth Heineman's "The Hour of the Woman: Memories of German's 'Crisis Years' and West German National Identity."[5] And we have books such as the study of Asunción Lavrin, *Women, Feminism, and Social Change in Argentina, Chile, and Uruguay, 1890–1940*,[6] a work that studies the history of feminism in the three South American countries mentioned in the title. These are topics that would have made conventional male historians of a century ago tremble in horror, but today they occupy an honored and fascinating place in serious research. In a similar way historians study the role of people of African descent in many societies, the history of immigrants, labor history, sexual history, the history of fashion, the history of sports. All these and more demonstrate interests of historians toiling to uncover as much of the human experience as possible and leading the profession of history itself away from the notion that to understand the past we need only understand the personalities and decisions of a few white male leaders.

Whatever its subject, the study of history is an unending detective story. Historians try to solve mysteries in the evidence and to tell a story that will give order to the confusion of data we inherit from the past. Historians make connections, assign causes, trace defects, make comparisons, uncover patterns, locate dead ends, and find influences that continue through the generations until the present.

We encounter history by reading and writing. We read books and articles, and slowly we gain some understanding of the shape of the past,

[5]*AHR* (April 1996): 395.
[6]Lincoln: University of Nebraska Press, 1995.

the general framework within which events took place. When we study history in college, we write about the past using the methods of professional historians. Writing helps us think about what we know, and of course it helps our instructors see what we know and how we think.

This little book will guide you through some major steps in writing papers in history for college undergraduate classes. It is a book both about methods in historical study and about methods in writing. It should help you gain some understanding of general problems underlying all historical study, and it should help your writing in all courses that you take in the college or university. It should also make you a better detective and a better teller of some of the innumerable stories that taken together make up the study of the past.

Most of the book will deal with research you can conduct in your own college library or on the Internet. A brief section will also explain how to take notes and how to use those notes to do well on both research papers and on exams you may take in a history course.

1

The Essay in History

We saw in the introduction that history is far more than an assembly of facts. It is the writer's interpretation of facts that raises questions, provokes curiosity, and makes us ask the questions *who, what, where, when,* and *why*. The writer's interpretation adds up to what we call a "thesis," a point of view that binds everything in an essay together.

This chapter gives a checklist to help you study your writing about history to see if it conforms to the expectations readers of history bring to books and articles. Readers typically bring to your writing expectations they have formed by reading other books and articles about history. Don't disappoint them. Guide your own work by the following standards.

1. The historical essay has an argument.

We write essays about history to interpret something we want readers to know about the past. We provide data—information from our sources, our evidence—and our argument about what the facts mean.

"Argument" here does not mean angry, insulting debate as though anyone who disagrees with you is a fool. Rather, it is the main thing the writer wants to tell his or her readers, the reason for writing the essay. It is the thesis of the paper, the proposition that the writer wants readers to accept. A good historical essay quietly expresses the thrill of a writer's discovery. You cannot have that thrill yourself or convey it to others if you do nothing but repeat what others have said about your topic. Don't be content with telling a story others have told hundreds of time, the sort of story you might copy out of an encyclopedia whose aim is to give you the facts, the facts, and nothing but the facts. Find something puzzling in the evidence, and try to solve the puzzle or to explain why it is a puzzle. Ask a question and try to answer it.

2. Good historical essays have a sharply focused, limited topic.

You can develop a thrill of discovery *only* if you limit your topic sufficiently to let you study and think about the sources carefully. Find a topic you can manage in the time and space you have available.

Most unsuccessful history papers, in my experience, fall short because the writer has chosen a subject no one can possibly treat in a paper of the sort generally required in undergraduate history courses. An 18-year-old student of mine several years ago wanted to write a psychoanalysis of Henry VIII in seven pages. England's Henry VIII was a complex and unpleasant man, as any one of his six wives and numerous mistresses might have testified. If a modern psychiatrist with degrees in medicine and psychotherapy put Henry on the couch and interviewed him week after week, two or three years would pass before the psychiatrist would feel capable of making a judgment about Henry's character and motives. A student with no training in psychiatry and no knowledge of the thousands of pages written about this bizarre and savage king cannot say anything worthwhile on so broad a topic.

Here is a lesson to brand in fire across any young historian's mind: If you try to do too much, you will not do anything. To write a good essay in history you must be sure that evidence is available, that you have time to study it carefully and repeatedly, and that you choose a topic on which you can say something worthwhile. Some of my students have written papers such as these: "A Study of the Prejudices against Blacks and Women in the 1911 Edition of the *Encyclopaedia Britannica*"; "Ten Years of Opinions by Historians on the Value of *The Age of Jackson* published by Arthur M. Schlesinger, Jr., in 1945"; "How a Confusion in Orders Caused the British Disaster in the Battles of Lexington and Concord on April 19, 1775"; "A Comparison of the Use of Shakespeare in Kenneth Branagh's Filming of *Henry V* with That of Lawrence Olivier." All these papers depended on sources the writers could study carefully in the time available before the papers were due. It is always a good idea to discuss paper topics with your instructor. Sometimes a brief conversation can sharpen a topic so that your paper will become a genuine exploration of an interesting subject.

3. Good papers in history are based on primary sources.

Primary sources are texts nearest to any subject of investigation. Secondary sources are always written *about* primary sources. Primary sources for an essay about the Mexican revolutionary Emiliano Zapata early in this century would be letters and speeches of Zapata himself. Secondary sources would be books and articles by scholars such as John Womack and Samuel Brunk who have made careers of studying Zapata's movement and his assassination. For a paper about Woodrow Wilson as historian, Wilson's *History of the American People* is a primary source, as are the class notes he used for his lectures at Bryn Mawr and Princeton when he taught history at those colleges. Secondary sources would include essays and books by historian Arthur S. Link who made his career studying Wilson's presidency.

The most common primary sources are written documents. My student who wanted to examine attitudes towards blacks and women in the much praised 1911 Edition of the *Encyclopaedia Britannica* had read an article in *The New Yorker* magazine about this famous edition, noted for its clear writing and careful drawings illustrating the engineering marvels of the day. The *New Yorker* article commented on the encyclopedia's racist assumptions. My student wanted to see for herself not only what the 1911 edition said about race, but how it treated women. She studied articles on the "Negro," on Africa, and on various issues relating to women, and she considered what kind of women were deemed worthy to make the pages of this work. The article in *The New Yorker* was a secondary source; the primary source was the encyclopedia itself, and it was available in several sets in our university libraries.

Primary sources can also include photographs, paints, sculpture, architecture, oral interviews, statistical tables, and even geography. Professor Liana Vardi's fine article in the *AHR* of December 1996, entitled "Imagining the Harvest in Early Modern Europe," considers representations of peasants by artists for three centuries after 1500. She shows that gradually the peasants, the farmers who worked the fields, disappear from paintings of rural landscapes. By comparing paintings with poetry from the time, she argues that city dwellers and aristocrats became afraid of peasants, who frequently revolted against the harsh conditions of their lives. Then in the eighteenth century peasants returned to paintings, where they appear docile and obedient and happy. The paintings, which are reproduced in black and white throughout the article, serve as an essential primary source. You, too, can find important visual sources for papers you write in college classes.

Never forget the power of the interview in writing about history. If you write about any historical event of the past sixty or seventy years, you can with a little effort find somebody who participated in it. Participants may be delighted to share their stories with you. And their stories can illuminate major social movements in the country as a whole. Did a strike take place at a paper mill in your Maine town some years ago? Go interview some of the strikers and some mill managers to supplement what you read on the subject. Consult old newspaper and perhaps magazine files for stories about the strike that will help you ask questions.

Always remember in an interview that participants can get things wrong. Human beings forget, or they tell the story in such a way to exalt themselves, and sometimes they simply lie. The historian is always skeptical enough to check out the stories he or she hears, even from eyewitnesses.

My great aunt Doll died in 1945 when I was a child. She used to tell us stories of how she and my grandmother, her sister who died before I was born, had hidden under a cherry dropleaf table in the farm house where they lived in East Tennessee during the Civil War while Federal troops skirmished with Confederates across the yard. The men in the family, except for the youngest son, were all away serving in the Federal army, and Aunt Doll could tell a thrilling tale of the skirmish, the bullets whistling through the windows and thunking into the wooden sides of the house. Much later I discovered that she had been born early in 1862, that the skirmish had been in November 1863, and that it is very doubtful that she could have remembered it.

Although primary sources are basic to history, secondary sources are also essential. You should always consult books and articles written by historians about the subject you write about yourself. These books and articles will help you learn how to think about history, and they will provide much information that you can use. I'll say more about secondary sources later on.

4. Write your history paper in the same spirit that you would tell a good story.

As I said in the introduction, a good story begins with something out of balance, some tension to be received or explained. Or you can say that a good story begins with a problem. Here is a beginning that works:

"The whole affair was mismanaged from first to last." So wrote British Lieutenant John Barker in his diary after he survived the battles of Lexington and Concord on the first day of fighting in the American Revolution. Why did well-trained professional British soldiers meet with such a disastrous defeat at the hands of disorganized American farmers called "minutemen"? Barker had one answer—the ineptitude of his own British commanders.

The writer gets to the point quickly by quoting Barker and revealing a tension that we want to see resolved. Seeing the quotation, we ask questions: "How was the affair mismanaged?" "Was Barker right?" "How could the British have avoided defeat that day?" The beginning puts various elements together, reveals tension, makes us ask questions, and proceeds. A paper on ideas can begin the same way. The writer should introduce the tension in the subject quickly and set out to explain its importance.

The main quality of any story is that it makes us relive the experience it describes. We feel cheated standing in line to be admitted to a mystery movie if a kid coming out shouts at us, "The girlfriend did it." We say to friends who have seen a movie we plan to see, "Don't tell me how it ends." We want to live through the experience for ourselves. A good writer creates the experience of living through events or of living through a step-by-step interpretation of those events.

The experience of the movie is not exactly like our experience in historical writing. Later on I shall suggest that when you pick up a history book to use in your research, you read the last chapter before you read the book to see where the historian is going. Still, any good piece of writing leads us through a process of discovery, providing information that lets us follow the writer's lead and arrive finally at the climax, where everything comes together. In a good essay or book about history, we can know how the story comes out and still appreciate the art of the historian in getting us to that conclusion. We read not only to know how things come out but also to know how they happen.

Writers of history papers should not give us surprise endings. Inexperienced writers often fall into the temptation of withholding necessary information or otherwise distracting us to prevent us from guessing where they are going. Such tactics are annoying, and professional historians don't use them. The climax in a history paper is usually a place where the last block of information is fitted in place and the writer's case is proved as well as his or her knowledge permits. The paper closes shortly after the climax because once the case is proved, a summary of the significance of the events or ideas described may be all that is necessary.

5. Get to the point quickly.

A good essay sets the scene quickly, reveals a tension to be resolved, and sets out in the direction of a solution. Some writers take so long to introduce their essays that readers lose interest before they get to the writer's real beginning. Some writers shovel out piles of background information or long accounts of previous scholarship in a somewhat frantic effort to prove that the writer has studied the issue. Or we may get some sort of moral justification for the topic, implying something like this: "I am writing this paper to make a better world and to prove that I am on the right side." The best writers have something to say and start saying it quickly. Readers should know your general subject in the first paragraph, and within two or three paragraphs they should usually know why you have written your essay.

Often an apt quotation from a source provides a launch pad that allows the writer to get quickly into the subject at hand. Look at the quotation from a Chinese Emperor that historian Joanna Waley-Cohen uses in her article, "China and Western Technology in the Late Eighteenth Century" and how she uses it to introduce her subject:

> "We have never valued ingenious articles, nor do we have the slightest need of your country's manufactures."

Having given us this quotation, Professor Waley-Cohn proceeds with the essay:

> By the late eighteenth century, the balance of European opinion had tilted against China. Westerners, earlier in the century almost uncritical in their admiration, came to the conclusion that the Chinese seemed unwilling, or unable, to improve on their earlier inventions, such as gunpowder and the compass, which formed part of the foundation for Western development. The famous assertion of Chinese self-sufficiency quoted above, made in 1793 by the Qianlong emperor (r. 1736–1795) in response to Lord Macartney's embassy from King George III, seemed to epitomize Chinese aloofness to the potential offered by Western knowledge.
>
> Europeans especially equated this apparent lack of interest in what the West had to offer with a lack of interest in science and practical technology, because at that time the West had come to define itself in terms of, and derive a strong sense of superiority from, its undoubted technological power. From such a perspective, it was an easy step to regarding the Chinese as inferior in an overall sense. These views took firm hold as the nineteenth century unfolded and have remained tenacious to this day. Although scholars have recently exploded the myth of China's "opposition" to Western science, it remains widely believed, and, in the case of technology, neither the conviction of the Chinese lack of interest or the assumptions on which it rested have been subjected to serious inquiry.
>
> Yet the situation in the eighteenth century was far more complex than Qianlong's public declaration suggests. In the preceding decades, he and a number of others in China had displayed considerable interest

in all manner of things Western, particularly science and technology. Although this interest was duly recorded by a range of Western observers and made widely available to their European readers, the overwhelming body of opinion disregarded that evidence in favor of the attitudes outlined above.[1]

We can tell from this opening that Professor Waley-Cohen will attack the standard opinion about China and technology, and so she does. Try to be as direct as she is.

Once you have begun, don't digress. Stick to the point. Be sure everything in your paper serves your main purpose, and be sure your readers understand the connection to your main purpose of everything you include. Don't imagine that you have to put everything you know into one essay. An essay makes a point. It is not an excuse to pour out facts as if you were dumping the contents of a can onto a tabletop.

6. Write a good title for your paper.

A good title, sometimes supplemented by a subtitle, informs your reader and helps keep you on track as you write. Always provide a title to your own essays, and make it represent the contents of the essay as clearly as possible. Historians sometimes use a colon in their titles. Here is the title of an influential article by Hanna Holborn Gray in the 1963 *Journal of the History of Ideas:* "Renaissance Humanism: The Pursuit of Eloquence." Readers know immediately that the article is to be about Renaissance humanism, defined here as "the pursuit of eloquence." Go from a clear title to the purpose of your paper as quickly as you can. Titles, subtitles, and opening paragraphs should fit together as a unit. Remember that the title not only helps your reader know what you are talking about; it also helps you be certain you have defined a subject clearly. If you cannot write a succinct title for your work, you may not have a clear point to make in the essay itself.

7. Build your essay step by step on evidence.

You must give readers reasons to believe your story. Your readers must accept you as an authority for the essay you present to them. You cannot write history off the top of your head, and you cannot parade your opinions unless you support them. Nobody cares about your opinions if you don't know anything or if you don't take the trouble to tell us what you do know.

[1]*AHR* (December 1993): 1525–1526.

Writing about history is much like proving a case in a court of law. A good lawyer does not stand before a jury and say, "My friends, I firmly believe my client is innocent. You must believe he is innocent because I say he is. I feel totally convinced that he is innocent. You may think he is guilty. I disagree. I feel in my bones that he is innocent. I want you to rule that he is not guilty because in my opinion he is not guilty. Take my word for it." Clients with such lawyers should prepare themselves to spend a long time away from home in undesirable company. A bad lawyer may repeat himself. He may shout and weep and whisper and swear to the sincerity of his feelings. But the jury will not believe him unless he can produce some evidence.

So it is with the historical essay. Your readers are judge and jury. You are the lawyer arguing your case. It is all very good if your readers think you are sincere or high-minded or even eloquent. It is much more important that you convince them that you are right. To do that you must command your evidence and present it clearly and carefully.

What is evidence? The issue is complicated. Evidence is detailed factual information from primary and secondary sources. You must sift through these sources, decide what is reliable and what not, what is useful and what not, and how you will use these sources in your work. Serious journalists follow a rule that historians can also use: When you make a generalization, immediately support it by quoting, summarizing, or otherwise referring to a source. Generalizations are unconvincing without the help of specific information to give them content.

Historians fit their evidence together to create a story, an explanation, or an argument. To have evidence at their command, they spend days in libraries, in museums, or wherever sources of evidence are to be found. You cannot manufacture evidence out of thin air; you must look for it. When you find it, you must study it until you know it almost by heart. If you make a careless summary of your evidence and get it wrong, you lose the respect of knowledgeable readers.

Evidence is everywhere. Sometimes people make spectacular discoveries of lost or forgotten documents. The discovery of the journals of James Boswell, the eighteenth-century companion and biographer of Samuel Johnson, was a remarkable event. They turned up in a Scottish castle where they lay scattered about like so much waste paper. The capture of German archives following World War II was momentous, allowing us to trace German political and military policy through this century and much of the last. The Freedom of Information Act has opened many

FBI and other government files that were long secret, and now the collapse of the Soviet Union has opened vast archives to scholars.

The papers of important men and women in history are often printed and published in great editions. I worked for years on the *Yale Edition of the Complete Works of St. Thomas More* published by Yale University Press. Now every student of Thomas More can find in these twenty volumes almost every surviving item that More wrote. The papers of American presidents are being steadily published. The papers of Woodrow Wilson have been published by Princeton University Press in sixty-eight large volumes. The papers of Andrew Johnson are appearing from the University of Tennessee Press. Many college libraries have these and other presidential papers, and if your college does not possess them, you may get them on interlibrary loan.

The letters and papers of men and women, famous and obscure make fascinating records of their times, and many collections have been published from the classical age to the present. Both the diary and letters of the English writer Virginia Woolf have been published in many volumes and offer an intimate view of her important career. Letters and journals make fascinating reading, especially if they cover long periods of time, and they are gold mines for the historian. You can pick a subject and follow the writer's thoughts on it, or activity in events related to the subject, and have an excellent paper for a college history course.

Sources of local history abound in courthouses, old newspapers (often preserved on microfilm), diaries, letters, tax records, city directories, the recollections of older people, and myriad other papers. These sources can provide details, often small ones, that can make the past come alive in a moment. I worked afternoons on a small newspaper when I studied journalism at the University of Tennessee. I hit on the idea of writing a column about the history of our rural county, interviewing older people and looking at old records wherever I found them. Two elderly women allowed me to use the diary of their father, sheriff of our county in 1883 when the last public hanging took place on our courthouse lawn. The man hanged was named Andrew Taylor, and he had not only robbed a train but had also shot the engineer and driven the train into our town before making his getaway on horseback. The sheriff went after him with a posse, captured him in a cave, and brought him back for trial and execution. I was able to find newspaper files from that time. They gave me yet another view of the trial. I even found a very old man living in a cockroach-infested rented room who as a child had seen Andy Taylor bring the train into the railroad station and gallop away. "I remember he was wearing red socks," the old man told me—a detail that somehow made the whole mad scene become more vivid. I wrote a story for my paper that would have done just as well in a history class.

Historians and their readers love evidence. They love telling details. They love old things. They immerse themselves in evidence—both primary and secondary sources—see its patterns, and write about them. To try to write a good paper without evidence is like trying to ride up a mountain on a bicycle without wheels.

8. Document your sources.

Formal essays in history document their sources by means of footnotes, endnotes, or attributions written into the text. Readers want to know where you got your information. (Later in this book we'll discuss various modes of documentation.) You gain authority for your own work if you demonstrate that you are familiar with the primary sources and the work of others who have studied the same material.

Documenting sources is the best way to avoid plagiarism, and plagiarism remains the unforgivable sin of any writer. Plagiarism is the act of presenting the thoughts or words of others as your own. It constitutes the ultimate dishonesty in writing, a theft of intellectual property that is never forgiven in the publishing world. Tennessee writer Alex Haley claimed that his book *Roots* came from his investigation into the history of his own ancestors who came as slaves from Africa. The book was made into a television mini-series that gripped millions of Americans when it was aired over 12 nights in 1977. Haley was charged with plagiarism and paid $650,000 in damages to the writer whose work he had copied. Further investigation by historians revealed that he had made up much of his evidence, and when he died in 1992, his reputation among scholars was in ruins. Leading black historians and writers usually ignore him, and when he is mentioned, "plagiarist" is often attached to his name. His sad example should be a warning to all writers to document their sources with care.

In colleges and universities the penalties for plagiarism are also severe. If you copy paragraphs out of an encyclopedia or another book or article, or if you don't credit ideas you have taken from other writers, and if your instructor discovers what you have done, he or she will never trust you again. In my university plagiarists are summoned before a disciplinary board and expelled for a year, and the plagiarism is recorded permanently on their records. Always put material you copy from your sources in quotation marks if you use it word for word in your essay as you found it in the sources. Always tell your readers when you summarize or paraphrase a source. Always give credit to ideas you get from someone else, even if you express those ideas in your own words.

You don't have to document matters of common knowledge. Martin Luther was born on November 10, 1483. The Japanese attacked Pearl Harbor in Hawaii on Sunday morning, December 7, 1941. Zora Neale Hurston wrote the novel *Their Eyes Were Watching God.* Pieces of information like these are common knowledge. They are not disputed. They are known to anyone who knows anything about these subjects.

But suppose you consider a complex topic such as the difference between a seminar and a lecture course in teaching history. You might easily find Bonnie G. Smith's article, "Gender and the Practices of Scientific History: The Seminar and Archival Research in the Nineteenth Century" published in the October 1995 issue of the *AHR.* If you use her data and her research on how seminars began and how they differed from the lecture courses that had gone on before them, the limitation of the historical profession to males, and the extraordinary difficulties of doing research in the nineteenth century, you must document your reliance on her work. You lose your honor and your reputation if you don't.

You may find that some ideas you get on your own are similar to those you read in secondary sources. You should then document those secondary sources and either in a footnote or in the body of your text point out the similarities and the differences.

9. Historical essays are written dispassionately.

Don't choke your prose with your own emotions. We identify with the people and the times we write about, and often in studying history our emotions are aroused. We judge people. We decide whether they were good or bad. The best way to convey these judgments is to tell what these people did or said. You don't have to prove that you are on the side of the angels. You can trust your reader. If characters you describe did terrible things, readers can see the evil if you give them the details. If characters did noble things, your readers can tell that, too, without any emotional insistence on your part. Describing the British retreat from Concord and Lexington on April 19, 1775, historian Louis Birnbaum lets the facts speak for themselves:

The mood of the British soldiers was murderous. They surged around houses along the route, instantly killing anyone found inside. Some of the regulars looted whatever they could find, and some were killed while looting by Minutemen who had concealed themselves in the houses. Houses with fires in the hearth were burned down simply by spreading the embers about. Generally, those homes without fires on the hearth escaped destruction because it was too time-consuming to start a fire with steel and flint. As the column approached Menotomy, the 23rd Regiment was relieved of rear-guard duty by the marine battalion. Colonial fire reached a bloody crescendo in Menotomy, and again British troops rushed house after house, killing everyone found inside, including an invalid named Jason Russell.[2]

The author could have said, "The criminal and bloodthirsty British soldiers acted horribly in what they did to those poor, innocent people, and these wicked British soldiers killed in the act of looting houses got what they deserved." But readers don't need such coercive comments, and they often resent them. If you present the details, you can trust your readers to have the right reactions. You waste time and seem a little foolish if you preach at them.

10. A historical essay should include original thoughts of the author; it should not be a rehash of the thoughts of others.

Essays are examples of reasoning. The most respected essays demonstrate an author carefully setting things in order and making sense of them. Do not disappoint your readers by telling them only what other people have said about your subject. Try to show them that by reading your work, they will learn something new or see old knowledge in a new light, one that you have shed on the subject by your own study and thinking.

One of the saddest things I found about teaching is the conviction of too many of my students that they have nothing fresh and interesting to say about their topics. They don't trust themselves. They cannot express a thought unless they have read it somewhere else. A reason for this lack of confidence is that some students insist on writing about large, general topics that other people have written about hundreds of times. Only a little searching will turn up evidence of topics that have seldom been writ-

[2]Louis Birnbaum, *Red Dawn at Lexington* (Boston: Houghton Mifflin, 1986), 184.

ten about. Such evidence exists in every college library. If you take the time to look, you too can turn up new information and shape papers that are new and original.

You may not find new facts, but you can think carefully about the facts at your disposal and come up with something fresh and interesting. You can see new relations. You can see causes and effects and connections that others have missed. You may reflect on motives and influences. You may spot places where some sources are silent. You can present your own conclusions, which have the weight of authority behind them.

Don't write a paper in the spirit of the child who builds a model airplane bought in a kit from a hobby shop. The child sticks together parts that someone else has designed until he or she produces a model that looks like the picture on the box. Some students go to the library looking for information on a broad subject like the beginnings of the Civil War and take a piece of information here and another piece there. They stick it all together without contributing anything of their own except manual dexterity. They retell a story that has been told thousands of times, and they do not present a thought that they have not read elsewhere. Why not instead read the speech Senator Jefferson Davis of Mississippi made in the United States Senate as he resigned to become president of the Confederacy? Explain in a paper his justification for secession—and see if you think he left something out. Then you have a thoughtful paper. Do not be happy until you shape a story that cannot be read in every encyclopedia or textbook in the field.

11. Always consider your audience.

No one can write to please or interest every possible reader. Different essays are intended for different audiences. Every beginning history student should spend a few hours in the library looking at different periodicals devoted to history. It is fairly easy to spot publications devoted to specialists. *Renaissance Quarterly* is addressed to scholars who know a lot about the Renaissance and who don't have to be filled in on lots of background information. *The American Historical Review* is addressed to a more general scholarly audience, and although its articles are specialized, they include information to help the rest of us understand the context of the topic. *American Heritage* and *History Today* are fine journals, aimed at readers with an educated interest in history who are not necessarily specialists. If you study these journals, you will begin to see how different the intended audiences are.

Always consider what your intended audience already knows. For most history courses, you should write for your instructor and other students who are interested in your topic but may not be specialists in the field. Define important terms. Give enough information to provide a context for your essay. Say something about your sources, but do not get lost in background information that your readers know already.

For example, if you write an interpretation of Martin Luther King, Jr.'s *Letter from Birmingham Jail* of 1965, you will bore readers and even offend them if you write as if they have never heard of Dr. King. In the same way, you don't inform your readers that Shakespeare was an English playwright or that Abraham Lincoln was a President of the United States. No writer can be entirely sure what an audience knows or does not know. Just as we convey to our readers an "implied author," so we write with an implied reader in mind, someone we think may read our work. So the best you can do is to imagine yourself as a reader and consider the sort of thing you might read and believe, and write accordingly. But it is not always an easy task. The main principle is that you must always be making decisions about what you need to tell your readers and what you think they know already.

I tell my students that they should write their essays so fully that if their friends or spouses picked one up, they could read it with the same understanding and pleasure they might find in an article in a serious magazine. The essay should be complete in itself. The important terms should be defined. Everyone quoted or mentioned in the essay should be identified—unless someone is well known to the general public. All the necessary information should be included. I like to imagine a friend picking up an essay and not being able to stop until he or she has finished the piece. And it is always a good idea to have some other person read your work and try to say back to you what he or she thinks you have said.

12. An honest essay takes contrary evidence into account.

Good historians try to tell the truth about what happened. If you study any issue long enough and carefully enough, you will form opinions about it. You will think you know why something happened, or you will suppose that you understand someone. Yet the evidence in history seldom stacks up entirely on one side of an issue, especially in the more interesting problems about the past. Different parts of the evidence contradict each other; using your own judgment about it all means that you must face such contradictions squarely. If you do not, knowledgeable readers may decide that you are careless, incompetent, or even dishonest.

President Woodrow Wilson is a hero to many liberals today, including many historians of an older generation. He conceived the idea of the League of Nations, the failed ancestor to the present United Nations, and he advocated a peace without vengeance after the horrors of World War I. Yet President Wilson treated black Americans as inferior, did not want them to have the vote in the South, and instituted segregation in the Federal Civil Service. How do we deal with this contradictory evidence? Given the abundant evidence of Wilson's racial attitudes in the Princeton edition of his papers, it is careless and even dishonest to portray him as a liberal saint without acknowledging this other side to his character and his political record.

Different historians interpret the same data in different ways. In highly controversial issues, you must take into account views contrary to your own. For example, if you should argue that Robert E. Lee was responsible for the Confederate defeat at the battle of Gettysburg in 1863, you must consider the argument of a number of historians that the blame should be laid at the feet of General James Longstreet, one of Lee's subordinates. You can still argue that Lee was the major cause of the Confederate disaster (although you should recall that the Federal army also had something to do with it). You don't weaken your argument by recognizing opposing views if you then can bring up evidence that supports your opinion against them. On the contrary, you strengthen your case by showing readers that you know what others have said, even if their opinions contradict your own. Readers will believe you if you deal with contrary opinions honestly, but they will scorn your work if you pretend that contradictions don't exist. This advice translates into a simple principle. Be honest. Nothing turns readers off so quickly as to suppose that the writer is not being fair.

Another principle is at stake here. History is not a seamless garment. Our knowledge of the past—or of almost anything else—has bumps and rips and blank spots that remain when we have done our best to put together a coherent account of it. Our best plan always is to approach the study of the past with the humility that rises from the experience of our ignorance.

13. Essays use standard English and observe the common conventions of writing.

Sometimes student writers feel abused when instructors require them to spell words correctly, use correct grammar and punctuation, and proofread their papers. But it is a terrible distraction to try to read a paper that does not observe the conventions. Readers want to pay attention to what a writer says. They do not want to ask questions like these: "Is that word spelled correctly?" "Why is a comma missing here?" "Why this word that does not fit the context?" Reading is hard work, especially when the material is dense or complicated, as it often is in history courses. A careless attitude towards the conventions may not bother writers because they think they know what they want to say. But it throws readers off.

Students who complain when instructors enforce the conventions do themselves a great disservice. In the world beyond college, few things about your writing will be more harshly judged than careless disregard for the conventions. We all would like to believe that our ideas are so compelling that no one can resist them, no matter how sloppily we write. Readers we seek to impress in a job application or in a report or letter will judge otherwise. Never hand in a paper without proofreading it carefully. Read it over and over to find misspelled words, lapses in grammar, typos, and places where you have inadvertently left out a word (a common error in these days of writing with the computer). Use the spell checker on your computer. But remember! The computer cannot replace the brain. The spell checker can tell you when a word does not appear in the dictionary, but it cannot tell you that you should not use "there" when you mean "their" or "shot" when you mean "shut."

14. Let your first and last paragraphs mirror each other.

The first and the last paragraphs of a good essay reflect some of the same words and thoughts. You can read these paragraphs and have a pretty good idea of what the intervening essay is about. An essay is somewhat like a snake biting its tail: The end always comes back to the beginning. You can see that mirroring of first and last paragraphs in the essay on fashion by Professor Mary Louise Roberts quoted in the introduction to this book. Study them carefully.

The end should not come back to the beginning in a mechanical way. It's a bit clumsy to begin an essay by saying, "In this essay I am going to do this, this, and this," and I find it boring to end an essay by saying, "I have done this, this, and this." Try to begin and end with more interesting statements. But however you begin, your first and last paragraphs should demonstrate some common words and thoughts.

These are some principles for good essays about history. Keep them in mind as you write your own.

2

Thinking about History

Writing history involves a special way of thinking related to a subject we discussed in the last chapter—telling a story. The past in all its complexity cannot be recaptured like an instant replay in televised sports. Real life has no instant replay. History does not repeat itself. The stuff of history—human experience—moves ceaselessly, changing endlessly in a process so complicated that it is like a turning kaleidoscope that never makes the same pattern twice.

Consequently, we know history only by the stories that are told about it, stories that are told by many people, supported by many different kinds of evidence, told in different ways in different times and in different places. Indeed in many languages the words for "history" and "story" are the same. Historical research and historical thinking always involve listening to a multitude of voices, mute perhaps on the page but speaking in our own intellect as we try to sort them all out and arrive at the story that is most plausible to us.

In modern times, a consciousness of history begins with the knowledge that present and past are different. In the past, the writing of history flourished when the historians realized that times were changing, that the new was replacing the old, and that the story of the old should be written down before it was lost. The speed of change in the daily life since the coming of the industrial revolution has been extraordinary. Therefore, it should not be surprising that the interest in history has grown in proportion as change has swept the past away.

To write history means to make an effort to tell the story of the past in language that makes sense to readers in the present. But the effort to make sense to readers in the present may distort the story. It is all a very difficult business! Yet it is necessary because the past has such power over us. We want to know how things got this way. We yearn to understand origins and purposes, and essential parts of our own lives in the present are influenced by our understanding of the past. At this writing, debate has been raised anew about the origin of an explosion that sank the U.S. battleship *Maine* in Havana Harbor in Cuba on February 15, 1898. At the time, American newspaper reports stirred public opinion to

29

believe that the *Maine* was sunk by a bomb planted against its hull by Spanish agents. Not long afterwards the United States declared war against Spain. American troops defeated the Spaniards in Cuba, Puerto Rico, the Philippines, and other territories, and the United States acquired an overseas empire for the first time. Now some evidence seems to suggest that a fire in a coal bunker in the ship itself ignited ammunition stored nearby, sinking the ship with the loss of almost 200 American sailors. Historical research into the origins of that now distant war serves to make many of us cautious when our government tells us today that we must go to war because our honor or our morals are in peril if we do not. And certainly no historians after the Vietnam War tell the story of the Spanish-American war as if the United States engaged in a holy crusade against evil back then. Present and past work together to condition our attitudes towards both of them.

What really happened? That is the fundamental question we would all like to know about the past. But the problems of history resemble the problems of memory. What were you doing a year ago today? If you keep an appointment book, you can find in it the names of people you saw that day. But what did you say to each other? If you keep a journal, you have a better record. But the journal does not tell you everything. Someone says to you, "I remember when we sat on the beach at Pawley's Island, South Carolina, year before last in August and talked about Elvis Presley's death." "Oh," you may say, "I thought that was three years ago in a cafe in Charleston." You may have recorded the conversation in your journal; or you may have forgotten to make an entry that day. So where did the conversation take place?

We have sources to use to check our own memories. Historians have their sources, too, as a check against the folk history, a sort of oral tradition that gets passed down among all people to describe their past. That oral tradition usually floats in myth and legend. The sources the historians use offer protection against the threat that the story of our past will be told finally by those with the loudest voices.

We have noted already that the sources for history have been conditioned by when they were created, and we are conditioned by our own times in how we read them. Legends of the saints told in the Middle Ages are filled with miraculous happenings. St. Denis was said to have been beheaded in Paris while preaching to the pagan Gauls; he walked with his head in his hands to the site that later became the monastery of St. Denis outside the city, and he set his head down there to mark the place where he should be buried. The kings of France were later buried in the monastery church built on the site. A statue of the saint, holding his head in his hands, stands now on the front of Notre Dame Cathedral in Paris. (It is a reconstruction of a statue torn down by mobs in the French Revolution.)

Most of us don't believe that people walk about holding their severed heads in their hands. We respect this tale as a charming legend, not literal truth. Did the people of medieval Paris believe the story of the miracle? In our supremely reasonable attitude towards the past, we may assume that the story of St. Denis was a good way for the bishops of Paris to emphasize the importance of their city and the truth of the orthodox Christian theology they professed. Paris achieved a sacred status because of the miracle. But who can tell? Maybe the bishops did believe the story, and perhaps we have to revise our nice, reasonable explanations for its origins.

And what happens when we apply our nice, reasonable explanations to a modern phenomenon such as Adolf Hitler? How could Hitler take over Germany? He devised a mad and passionate hatred of Jews and created in the Holocaust one of the great horrors of Western history. Could he do so because the Germans were historically more anti-Semitic than other European peoples and were waiting for someone like himself to put their hatred of the Jews into a program to exterminate them? Or was anti-Semitism a hateful virus infecting all European countries (and the United States), and did a collection of historical accidents bring Hitler to power and create the Holocaust? Could similar accidents have happened in other European powers so that any one of them might have been capable of the genocide that Hitler and the Germans imposed on the Jews? As I write this edition of this book, the debate rages furiously in historical books and journals and in the popular press.

The stories history tells are about human beings living in particular times and places. Human motives are in every age complex, mysterious, and often absurd. Many people in every land do crazy and destructive things for no reason that we can see, and scapegoats for national calamities or imagined enemies are summoned up by hysterical leaders to be blamed and to have horror inflicted upon them. "Rational" people cannot believe St. Denis walked across Paris carrying his severed head in his hands. But how could "rational" people also acquiesce in Hitler's plans for Germany?

All this is to say that history involves us both in modes of thought common to the daily life and in the effort to understand acts and ideas utterly foreign to our own. We must weigh evidence, deciding what to believe and what not, what we know and what we think is probable or at least plausible. We tell stories about what happened. We try to discover what it all means—and in so doing try to understand better what it is to be a human being.

We begin to think creatively in the study of history by questioning our sources. In the rest of this chapter we shall see how that questioning may go on.

QUESTIONING YOUR SOURCES

Good papers are built on primary sources, but secondary sources are essential to the historian's task, and you should always use them. The trick is not to follow slavishly the materials you find in secondary sources. Use them to add to your own knowledge and to help you shape your own questions about the material.

When you are considering a topic, your first step should be to go to the reference room in your library and read articles about it in many different encyclopedias. The articles in good encyclopedias are written by experts who summarize the state of knowledge about a subject at the time they write. They give you an overview that can provide a context for your own later work. Reading various encyclopedia articles without taking notes your first time through is a little like looking down from an airplane to a landscape you want to explore. When you get back on the ground, you will choose only a part of that landscape to study, but it is helpful to see the larger shape and context of the area where you will focus your own efforts.

Then read articles in news magazines and newspapers from the time you are writing about, if such sources exist for your topic. (You will not find newspapers from the Middle Ages!) Look up important words in dictionaries. Consult the various bibliographies now available on CD-ROM or in the online catalogues in your library. Look through promising books and articles about your topic. Ask reference librarians where to look for information. Following these steps will give you a feel for your subject and the general state of knowledge about it. The time you spend in this preliminary reading will save you hours as you work later on with your paper.

At some moment, however, you must go to primary sources and study them thoroughly. If you want to write a paper on Woodrow Wilson's racial attitudes, go to the Wilson papers and use the index in each volume to direct you to Wilson's thoughts on various subjects related to your topic.

Read with the journalistic questions in mind—*who, what, where, when,* and *why.* It's a good idea to jot those questions down in your notes and to try to answer them briefly as you read. They will help you sort things out and organize your approach to the topic. The questions correspond to an almost universal way that literate people respond to information. When something happens, we ask who the people involved were, what exactly happened, when it happened, where, and why. The answers often overlap. It may be impossible to separate a *what* question from a *why* question. To explain *what* happened is sometimes to explain *why* it happened. We can scarcely separate a *who* question from a *what* question. To talk about someone is to discuss what that person did.

The overlap of questions is the very reason journalists use them. A complex event is like an elaborate tapestry tightly woven of many different-colored threads. The threads are distinct, but they are hard to sort out. The journalistic questions help keep our eyes on this or that important thread so we can see how it contributes to the whole. They help us analyze human actions.

In police investigations (and in mysteries) detectives look for motives. Why was the murder committed? Suspicion falls on those who had some reason to kill the victim. Yet to establish an obvious motive is not to prove that the person who benefits most from the death was the killer. In any historical event, we look at those who benefited from it and at those who were hurt by it. And we look for the irrational. Some people in our society get shot to death by stray bullets, and a number die in quarrels over traffic accidents. Impulse sometimes changes the world. Racial segregation in the federal civil service—including the U.S. Post Office— came about during the administration of President Woodrow Wilson shortly after he took office in 1913. That is what happened. Who was responsible? Who influenced Wilson? Who was affected? Who protested? Why was segregation installed? When was it done? Where was it carried out? The emphasis we place on this or that journalistic question may determine the approach we take to writing an essay about a historical event. We might write one essay about Wilson's racial attitudes, and another quite different essay on segregation in the federal civil service and its relation to segregation in state and local governments in America.

The journalistic questions can help you work through writer's block. All of us experience writer's block at one time or another. We cannot get started, or we cannot go on, or we cannot finish. If you write out the journalistic questions and various answers to them, you can give your mind a push that starts an engine going in your head. *Writing stimulates the mind. Almost any process that makes you write about the topic of your essay will fill your mind with thoughts you could not have had if you had not started writing first.*

Remember that each journalistic question can be posed in many different ways. There is not one *who* question or one *what* question or one *why* question. There may be dozens. Ask as many of them as you can. Push your mind.

"Who" Questions

Who was Pearl Buck? When did she live? Why is she famous? Where did she live? What did she do? Whom did she write about? Who loved her work? What did her missionary experience in China do to affect her view of that country? What books and articles did she write? What did she do to influence American attitudes towards China? Why did she win the Nobel Prize? When was the prize given to her? What did literary critics say about her work? Who were some of these critics? What did her fans say about her? Who were some of these important fans? What do people say about her work now? Who are some of these people? When did the attitude about her work begin to change? Why did it change? Who was influential in making it change?

As you ask such questions, jotting down brief answers—or noting that you don't know the answers—you suggest many topics, and your thought evolves. You begin to see relations between some of your questions. For example, you may push yourself to ask a dozen or more *where* questions or a multitude of *why* questions. We know that American public opinion was shocked when the Communists under Mao Zedong took over the Chinese mainland in 1949. Many politicians, including Senator Joseph McCarthy of Wisconsin, claimed that the United States had "lost" China for democracy because the U.S. Department of State was infested with Communist agents. Now such talk seems silly at best and malicious at worst. Did Pearl Buck's idealistic books about China, especially her classic *The Good Earth,* help create an unreal impression of the situation there? Questions such as these can lead you to Buck's books, to reviews of her work in her own time, and to articles about her since. From them you can find your way to a good essay.

So you should jot down as many questions under each category as you can think of. The *who* question can make you think about biography, about responsibility, about the actors in historical events, and about those whom they affect. Sometimes the *who* question can help satisfy simple curiosity. Who was involved in the English Bloomsbury group of writers early in this century, a group that turns up in many articles about literature in that time? Who was responsible for the Watergate burglary that caused Richard Nixon to resign from the Presidency?

"What" Questions

The *what* question may involve weeding out legends and misunderstandings to see what *really* happened. Who fired the first shot on April 19, 1775, when British soldiers faced a ragged line of American colonials in the skirmish that began the American Revolution? Another *what* question asks, "What does this mean?" Here we try to see what people in the past meant by the words they used. These meanings can confuse us because they often change.

In the nineteenth century the word *liberal* was used to describe businessmen who wanted to make a place for themselves in a country ruled by an aristocracy with its power based on land. The liberals were capitalists who thought government ought to keep its hands off business. Most liberals believed that the economy ran by implacable laws of supply and demand and that any effort to help working people interfered with those laws and was bound to lead to catastrophe.

In the twentieth century, the word *liberal* has been used by Americans to describe those who want government to hold the balance of power between the strong and the weak, the rich and the poor. At this writing neither political party wants to use the word because it implies spending by the government for programs to help the poor and the weak, and consequent taxes to support that spending.

What relations exist between the use of the words in these different ways? Liberals in both the nineteenth and twentieth centuries have advocated "liberty," the root word of *liberal.* Nineteenth-century liberals wanted to create liberty for the business classes who suffered under custom that gave political power to landed aristocrats. Twentieth-century liberals have tried to create more liberty for the poor, including the liberty to have a public school education with its recognition of talent and opportunities for advancement.

When you use such broad terms in your writing, you must define what you mean by them. Be on guard against reading today's definition into yesterday's words. Do not rely on simple dictionary definitions. Words are defined by their context in time and place, and you must be sure to understand their context.

"When" and "Where" Questions

When and *Where* questions often illuminate tricky puzzles in history. Sometimes we know exactly when and where something happened. We know the moment the first Japanese bombs fell on Pearl Harbor, the moment Franklin Roosevelt died, and exactly where the Confederate charge reached its high-water mark on the third day of the battle of Gettysburg. But asking when something happened in relation to something else can provide a fascinating topic of research. We do not know when Richard Nixon first learned that members of his White House staff were involved in the Watergate burglary of June 17, 1972. When did Israel leave Egypt in the Exodus described in the Bible? Several dates have been argued. Different dates mean different chronologies for Israel's relations with other nations in the region and for the development of Israel's history. When did volcanic eruptions destroy Minoan civilization on Crete? The question is related to the rise of power on the Greek mainland under states such as Athens and Sparta. When did Woodrow Wilson first express himself in opposition to the aspirations of American blacks? Was it an attitude thrust upon him by others when he became President, or had he opposed black progress before he entered politics?

Questions about where things happened can often be absorbing. No one knows exactly the location of the Rubicon River. Julius Caesar crossed it with his army in violation of a law of the Roman Republic that forbade the army to approach near the capital. But wherever it was, it has another name today. We know that the Rubicon was in North Italy and that it formed the border between the Roman province known as Cisalpine Gaul and the Roman Republic itself. But we don't know which modern Italian river was then called the Rubicon. Deciding where the Rubicon was might help us understand how much warning the Roman Senate had when Caesar moved with his troops on the capital.

Where questions involve geography, and geography often makes *where* questions overlap with *why* questions. Where are the rivers of the Netherlands? The rivers of France? The rivers of Africa? Where are mountains in every continent? Where are mountain passes? Various historians have argued that the rivers of France and the Netherlands provided a natural unity to those countries, whereas the rivers of Germany flow in such a way as to cause Germany to remain disunited. Some have argued that the geography of Africa makes unity of the African continent almost impossible. Where were the first railroads built? A glance at a map of railroads in the United States before 1861 reveals that it was much easier for people in my native East Tennessee to communicate with Washington and New York than it was for them to get to Charleston, South Carolina. Did this railway connection with the North help prepare East Tennesseans to take the firm stand for the Union that they assumed when the war broke out? Perhaps.

Think about geography when you write. Geography may not yield anything special for your work, but if you ask the right questions, geography may open a door in your mind onto a hitherto unimagined landscape of events and explanation. The Annales school of history in France made geography one of its fundamental concerns, asking such questions as how long it took to travel from one place to another in Europe, what the major trade routes were, where different crops were grown, what cities had the closest relations to one another, and so on.

For all historians, a good topographical map showing roads, rivers, mountains, passes, coasts, and location of towns remains an indispensable resource. The late Hajo Holborn, a professor of history at Yale, used to say that disputes often arise because statesmen draw boundaries along mountain crests or along rivers that can be defended in war. But, he said, in times of peace, the same people settle on both sides of a mountain pass and on both banks of a river so that a military boundary becomes an ethnic division. This principle makes it easier to understand many conflicts that have bloodied recent history.

The Importance of Asking "Why" Questions

Sometimes we know what happened, but why did it happen, and why did it have the influence it did? These questions about cause and effect create an eternal fascination and lead us to discuss one of the most important topics in the study of history—cause and effect. Cause and effect are like unruly twins. In historical study they are inseparable, but it is often difficult to see just how they relate to each other. Keep in mind several considerations.

1. Always distinguish between the precipitating cause and the background causes of a great event.

You might call the precipitating cause the triggering cause, the cause that sets events in motion. The background causes are those that build up and create the context within which the precipitating cause works.

Precipitating causes are often dramatic and fairly clear. Background causes are more difficult to sort out and often ambiguous. The precipitating cause of the Civil War was the bombardment and capture of Fort Sumter by the forces of South Carolina on April 12, 1861. President Lincoln immediately called for 75,000 volunteers to suppress the rebellion, and soon afterward fighting began. No one would claim that the incident in Charleston Harbor all by itself caused the Civil War. Behind the events of that Friday morning were complex differences between North and South—slavery in the Southern states, differences in economies, cultures, values, political philosophies, religious expressions, educational systems, different histories, and finally the 1860 election of Lincoln, who was known to oppose the extension of slavery in the territories west of the Mississippi River. These were background causes of the war, and ever since, historians have been trying to sort them all out to tell a sensible and precise story to explain why America's bloodiest war came.

Background causes offer rich possibilities for writing about the *why* of history. They allow writers opportunities for research, analysis, and conjecture. They often figure in serious newspaper reports trying to explain events that suddenly make headlines. The triggering cause makes the news; journalists and historians rush to explain the background causes that created a state of affairs where the triggering cause could work. If you pull the trigger of an empty pistol, you get only a snap of the firing pin. The pistol must be loaded before it will fire. Background causes are, in effect, the cartridge loaded in the gun that makes the trigger do something important. Historians write books and articles on such subjects—as thousands of historians have written on the background causes of the Civil War.

Precipitating or triggering causes can be worthwhile subjects in themselves. Exactly what happened at Fort Sumter on that April day in 1861? Why was it that passions were so aroused on that particular day in that particular year? The *what* question and the *why* question come together—as they often do.

2. Remember that historical causation is complex.

It is almost always a mistake to lay too much responsibility for a happening on only one cause. Rebecca West in her remarkable book about

Yugoslavia published in 1942, *Black Lamb, Grey Falcon,* tells in detail the story of the assassination of the Archduke Franz Ferdinand of Austria-Hungary in Sarajevo on Sunday, June 28, 1914—the precipitating cause of World War I.

The Archduke was heir to the throne of the Austro-Hungarian Empire. When he was murdered, leaders of the Empire decided they must punish Serbia, the country in the Balkans the Austrians believed responsible for the terrorists who killed Franz Ferdinand and his wife. Russia defended Serbia because the Serbs were Slavs, akin to the Slavs in Russia. Germany defended Austria against Russia. When the Archduke was shot to death, a chain of events was set dragging across Europe that pulled the continent into war. West tells the story of the assassination in novelistic detail.

She also goes deeply into all the centuries of conflicts in this region. Her thick book tells a complex story of grievances that Austrians and Serbs built up against each other, culminating in the assassination and the subsequent war. By studying so many sources, West shows how easy it was for the murder of the Archduke to precipitate the war—and helps us understand better the bloody fighting between Serbs and Bosnians in 1993 and afterwards.

Good historical writing considers different but related causes for a great event. The study of history helps us see how many different influences work on what happens. Causes in history are like the tributaries to a great river. While a bad historian sees only the main channel of the largest stream, a good historian looks at the entire watershed and maps the smaller streams that contribute to the whole.

Good historians see things in context—often a large context of people and events surrounding what they seek to describe. Thinking in context means that we try to sort out and weigh the relative importance of various causes when we consider any important happening. The sense of context is especially important today, when historians have discovered the masses, the common people who must follow if others are to lead. Nineteenth-century historians thought that if we understood the leaders, we knew everything we needed to know about historical movements. But we now seek questions like these: What was happening to the English people under Queen Elizabeth I that made her more tolerant of religious diversity than former English monarchs had been? Why did a rebellion of Indian soldiers in the service of the East India Company in 1857 in Bengal lead to massacres of British settlers all over India, and why were the British able to persuade other Indians to unite with them to put down the

rebellion in horrifying atrocities committed on the rebels and their supporters? These questions lead us to investigations of mass culture, including the lives of people often scarcely literate who have left few written
records behind. Since it is hard to resurrect the life of the masses, the
problem of answering the *why* questions of history becomes complex and
uncertain. But these difficulties don't remove from historians the obligation to try to make sense of them.

3. Be cautious in your judgments.

Do not give easy and simple causes for complex and difficult problems. Do not argue that the Roman Empire fell only because Romans
drank water from lead pipes or that the South lost the Civil War only because Lee was defeated at Gettysburg, or that the American civil rights
movement was all the work of the Reverend Martin Luther King, Jr. All
these events were caused by complex influences. We become foolish
when we try to lay too much responsibility on one dramatic event or famous leader.

The caution should also extend to your judgments about motivation
in history. We know that the Roman Emperor Constantine legalized
Christian worship in the Roman Empire after about 313 A.D. Was he a
sincere Christian? Or did he see that the Christians were numerous and
possessed a strong organization that might help hold together his decay-
ing empire? Was he devout? Or was he cynical? Historians have come
down on both sides.

Motivations fascinate historians and their readers. Why did Franklin
Roosevelt not open the gates of America to Jews persecuted by the Nazis
under Hitler in the 1930s? Why did Thomas More die? Why did President Harry S. Truman decide to drop the atomic bombs on Japan in August 1945? Why did Mao lead the Chinese in their disastrous "Cultural
Revolution" of 1966–1969?

Some *why* questions may seem to have been answered. Yet an in-
quiring historian may look on the evidence again and discover another
possible answer that contradicts accepted wisdom. Of such stuff is revi-
sionism in history made. Why did the South suffer so much poverty in the
years after the Civil War? An earlier answer was "Reconstruction," the
supposedly merciless exploitation of the South by carpetbaggers from the
North. Now the prevailing opinion is that white Southerners themselves
with their one-crop economy, their resolve to suppress black citizenship,
and their unwillingness to support public education were responsible for
many of their own difficulties. The process of reconsideration goes on.

Careful study of the evidence may often turn up new possibilities about questions that seem to have been answered.

In considering matters of cause and effect, avoid common fallacies in historical reasoning. "Fallacies" are illogical arguments that pose as logical statements. You may be familiar with the term *straw man.* People set up straw men when they argue against positions their opponents have not taken or when, without evidence, they attribute bad motives to opponents. A historian might argue that the sixteenth century was marked by much skepticism in matters of religion. An opponent might unjustly argue in response that the sixteenth century could not have experienced religious skepticism because the scientific world view of Galileo and Newton was unknown—as if religious skepticism depended on a scientific world view. Worse, opponents might argue that because the historian was not religious himself, he wanted to find skepticism in the sixteenth century. Neither of these issues has anything to do with the original argument. They set up straw men, arguments that may be easily attacked, and so give the appearance of victory—except that they are beside the point.

By all means avoid the fallacy that comes wearing an elaborate Latin name—*post hoc ergo proper hoc.* The Latin means simply, "After this; therefore because of this," and it refers to the fallacy of believing that if something happens after something else, the first happening caused the second. In my youth I heard the evangelist Billy Graham declare in a very loud voice that paintings of homosexual and heterosexual sex on the walls of Pompeii showed that the Roman Empire fell on account of sexual promiscuity. Pompeii was destroyed by a volcanic eruption of Mt. Vesuvius in 79 A.D. The last Roman emperor in the West was deposed in 476 A.D. It would seem a bit extreme to say that because there was sexual license in the first century, Rome fell in the sixth. Historical causation is much more complicated than that.

A more subtle problem with this fallacy arises with events that are closely related although one does not necessarily cause the other. The stock market in New York crashed in October 1929. The Great Depression followed. The crash contributed to a lack of confidence that made the Great Depression a terrible trauma for Americans and Europeans. But it is a mistake to say that the crash caused the Depression. Both seem to have been caused by the same economic forces. It is in this sort of relation that it becomes most necessary to think out the various strands of causation and to avoid making things too simple.

Avoid the bandwagon fallacy, the easy assumption that because many historians agree on an issue, they must be right. Consensus by experts is not to be scorned. But experts can also be prone to prejudices. Francis Russell tells of the rush of hostility directed against him when he attacked the previous consensus on the Sacco-Vanzetti case. Great historical work has been done by people who went doggedly in pursuit of the evidence against the influence of the consensus. But be sure you have evidence when you attack a consensus. You won't get anywhere if all you have is a gut feeling. Unless you have evidence to support your ideas, you may end with a bad case of mental indigestion.

The Use of Inference

In our discussion of the journalistic questions, we have assumed the ability of the mind to *infer*. We manage our daily lives by making inferences. In the morning we see low, dark clouds piled in the sky, and when we leave home, we take along an umbrella. Why? We have seen such clouds before, and they have often meant rain. We infer by calling on past experience to interpret a present event or situation. We cannot always be certain that what we infer is true. Sometimes black clouds blow away quickly, leaving the skies clear so that we grumpily lug around a useless umbrella and maybe a raincoat all day long. But without inference we would have to reinvent the world every morning.

Historians infer some answers to all the journalistic questions. We strive to make sense of a document, to decide exactly what it is and if it is reliable, and to understand why it might have been written, when it might have been, where, and by whom. For centuries in the Middle Ages, people believed that a document called the *Donation of Constantine* had been written by the Emperor Constantine early in the fourth century when Constantine became a Christian. According to the document, Constantine was cured of leprosy by a pope, and in gratitude moved from Rome to Constantinople and gave rule in the West to the pope. The document was used to prove the superiority of popes over kings in Europe.

In the fourteenth century, an Italian named Lorenzo Valla began to ask some questions about the *Donation*. Why did none of the people around Constantine who wrote about him and his reign mention his attack of leprosy or the *Donation?* Why did the document use words that were not coined until centuries later? Why was it not quoted by anyone until about the ninth century? Why did it make many historical errors? Valla concluded that the work was a forgery, and his judgment has been accepted ever since. From the reasons I have noted, Valla inferred that the work could not have referred to an actual historical event and that it could not have been written in the time of Constantine.

The aim of inference is coherence. We try to fit everything we know into a plausible whole. We infer that the many people who wrote about Constantine during his lifetime would have noticed if he had fallen victim to leprosy and would have mentioned it in their histories. We infer that there is something fishy about documents that use words not coined until long after the purported age of the document. Suppose we read this sentence in the diary of a pioneer woman who supposedly crossed the plains on her way to California in 1851: "We are having a very hard time, and I know that Americans who drive through Nebraska in years to come on Interstate 80 will scarcely imagine what we have endured." Our heads would jerk up. We would immediately infer that something is seriously wrong with the claims of this document. Lorenzo Valla reached a similar conclusion about the *Donation of Constantine*.

Examples of inference abound in the writing of history on any subject. The French medievalist Jacques Le Goff has classified the standing of various jobs in the Middle Ages by noting jobs that the church refused to allow priests to hold. If a priest could not hold the job, Le Goff reasoned, it must be work generally scorned. He mentioned the jobs of innkeepers, owners of bathhouses, and jugglers among others.

Many scholars use wills as points of inference. Wills bequeathing possessions show what the maker of the will owned, and that information can in turn show things about the life that the person lived. Wills can show other things as well. In England, for example, we may get some indication of the degree of orthodox Catholic sentiment in the sixteenth century by looking at the religious formulae expressed in wills. If we have formulae mentioning the Virgin Mary and the saints, we infer strong Catholic sentiment. If we have formulae that mention only God and Christ, we infer some form of Protestantism.

The laws of any society provide a rich field for inference. Laws don't come out of thin air. They reflect the values of the people who make them, and they respond to conduct that runs counter to values in that society in that time. Laws are not made by just anybody, but by people with some kind of authority—economic, religious, military, or whatever. Usually the people who make laws can enforce their values on everyone else—but not always. We can infer the nature of authority by looking at laws, and we can see conduct that rulers assume runs against those values. By comparing laws and legal cases that come to the courts, we can often infer how strictly laws are enforced. Most cities and states have laws against littering, but not many citizens end up in court for throwing beer cans out the windows of cars on our highways. We may infer that the authorities think littering is bad but not bad enough to punish those who litter.

When you make an inference important to your study of the sources, you become a questioner. You don't read your sources passively. You read them actively, trying to fill in the gaps you always find in them.

STATISTICS

Statistical information has become a major source for writing history. Modern governments keep statistics with religious passion. The United States Census, taken every ten years, offers a wealth of information, and the Bureau of the Census in Washington is a temple of numbers. Other agencies, such as various polling organizations, collect statistics with the same avid compulsion.

Statistics require interpretation. By themselves, they tell us little. What we infer from them may tell us a great deal, but if we infer badly, we can make serious errors. To some students of history, statistics seem tedious; to others they are exciting and open new windows to the past. The statistical interest of historians has come about in part because statistics are available, in part because computers have made using them much easier, and in part because of a change in philosophy among historians themselves.

I have mentioned one of the changes in philosophy: Historians no longer believe that their most important subjects are great leaders—the heroes, the villains, the writers and speakers, the famous and the notorious. Many historians are now much more interested in the common people, the masses who have left us few direct records and whose names and personalities have been lost to history while the political and military leaders, the writers, the revolutionaries, the discoverers, and others get their names in the history books.

These masses have not vanished without a trace. By applying statistical reasoning to such records as we have, we can sometimes understand more clearly the successes and failures of the leaders as well as what we know of the evolution of societies. In her book *Life in Black and White: Family and Community in the Slave South*,[1] Professor Brenda E. Steven-

[1]New York: Oxford University Press, 1996.

son has studied black and white families in Loudon County, Virginia, before the Civil War when tobacco plantations formed the basis of the economy. Using court records and business ledgers, including those in which records of white plantation owners were kept, she has studied the effects of gender on the slave economy. At first black males predominated, but later black women began to be brought in, allowing slave families to develop. But then the white owners, strapped for cash as Virginia lost its markets for tobacco, began selling off children of slaves to the booming cotton economy of the deep South. Her statistics provide yet another window into the evils of a slave system where, as so often happens, the profit motive triumphs over more humane considerations.

The near worship of statistics by modern bureaucratic societies makes the task of the historian both easier and harder as we move towards the present. The task is more easy because statistical information nowadays is recorded in precise, accessible, and usable forms. We can know, for example, the predominant ethnic and economic composition of various voting precincts in the United States, and we can know how these precincts voted in various elections. We can analyze the difference in voting patterns between, say, an Italian Catholic precinct and a conservative Jewish precinct in a large American city such as New York or Boston. We may then infer what issues accounted for the differences and similarities. Analysis of the voting patterns of such precincts—an analysis made familiar by the media—helps us understand why one candidate won and another lost or why one may win and why another may lose.

The use of statistics to understand voting patterns only scratches the surface of the possible uses of statistical information by historians. The data gathered by the U.S. Bureau of the Census and by a myriad of government agencies allow us to infer many things about populations—whether they go to regular religious services or not and if so what kind, whether they practice birth control, whether they send their children to school, whether they go to college, how many times they move, how much family income they have, and so on. Private opinion polls by agencies such as the Gallup organization and the Nielsen Ratings of television open a world of tastes and preferences to the scrutiny of not only advertising agencies and politicians but of scholars. Much of this information can be found in the reference room of any large library.

But statistics have their dangers. What do we measure? And what do our measurements mean? One of the more controversial books based on statistics in recent years has been *Time on the Cross: The Economics of American Negro Slavery* by Robert William Fogel and Stanley L. Engerman—as the title indicates, an effort to see the face of slavery by looking at statistics left over from slave days before the Civil War. In reviewing the book, historian Oscar Handlin discussed the contention of the authors that the average age of slave mothers when they gave birth to their first child was 22.5 years. Handlin pointed out that Fogel and Engerman drew their data from wills probated in "fifty-four counties in eight Southern States between 1775 and 1865 which enumerated 80,000 slaves."[2]

Eighty thousand is a considerable figure. One might assume that statistical data drawn from such a sampling would have validity. But what about the significance the authors put on their finding that the average age of slave mothers was 22.5 years? The authors argued that slave mothers were mature women at the birth of their first child and that therefore they must have been married. This fairly late age for the first birth would indicate a stable family life. Yet that is not clear, although Fogel and Engerman used this evidence to infer that sexual promiscuity among slaves was limited and that family life was close and enduring. Handlin argues that such an elaborate conclusion cannot be drawn from the evidence.[3]

Handlin's thoughts about the work of Fogel and Engerman are worth pondering, for difficulties abound in using statistics. Sometimes the quantity of statistical information available may seem daunting. Anyone may feel overwhelmed by a project that can involve seemingly endless tables of numbers, charts, and graphs. The interpretation of statistics requires a high level of skill. Statistics as a discipline is substantial and complex, involving a rigorous introduction to the methods of interpreting statistics to make sense. Even with such instruction, errors in interpretation are common. Numbers may provide a comforting appearance of exactitude, but the appearance may not match the reality.

Statistics cannot measure the intensity of beliefs. In political campaigns, polls show what percentage of a sampling of voters favors this or that candidate. But do those supporters feel strongly enough about their favorites to vote for them or, in a national crisis, go out into the streets to demonstrate or even fight for them? Various polls throughout the 1960s showed that a majority of Americans supported the Vietnam War. But when those statistics were broken down, it was evident that a majority of young men of military age did not support the war and that once draft exemptions for college students were abolished, support for the war on

---

[2]Oscar Handlin, *Truth in History* (Cambridge: Harvard University Press, 1981), 211.

[3]Handlin, pp. 210–226. This is only part of the lengthy criticism Handlin directs against the use of statistics in *Time on the Cross*.

campuses dwindled to a small minority of students. Perhaps out of the vigor of youth, the minority that opposed the war held its convictions with much more intensity and seemed willing to risk much more for them.

Some questions go beyond the power of statistics to measure. Many critics of the quantitative method of writing history protest that its practitioners claim to know more about the past than they really do. Nothing takes the place, say the critics, of understanding history through the lively written words of those who participated in it. To these more humanistically inclined historians, statistics are skeletons without muscle and breath. The quantitative historians reply that the humanistic historians go on and on arguing over the same old things and that if statistics are often inexact, they provide important information that allows us to see shapes in the past we could not see without the numbers the statisticians present. No doubt statistics help us go where other sources will not allow us entry. How far they let us go remains debatable, and the debate will continue.

If you write an essay based on quantitative research, be sure that you have enough data and that you know enough about interpreting statistics to avoid obvious errors. Learn the correct terminology for statistical analysis. (You must know the difference between the median and the average, the significance of the bell curve, and you must have some idea of how a random sample is collected.) And do not be afraid to ask an expert. You probably have several people on your faculty who teach statistics in one form or another and who understand the pitfalls of statistical research. Go talk to one of them about your essay. He or she will probably be delighted with your interest, and you will be doing your part to break down the unfortunate barriers that tend to assert themselves between faculty and students in too many schools.

A good caution is never to claim too much for any methodology we use in the study of history. Statistics can unlock some historical puzzles— but only if the historian knows the limits of statistical analysis and operates within those limits. Polls regularly ask a sampling of Americans to name people they admire most. The President of the United States is always high on the list, as are various actors, athletes, and well-known religious figures such as the Pope and various Protestant evangelists. But a historian would be foolish to suppose that the results measured anything more than what the respondents think they should say to a stranger who asks them such a question. The person who says that he admires a selfless minister of religion more than anybody else might in secret envy the CEO who teetered on the edge of legality while he siphoned off a hundred million dollars from his company just before it went bankrupt.

Skepticism is one of the historian's finest qualities. Historians don't trust their sources, and they don't trust their own first impressions. They question everything. They test their own insights and their own methods and motives. They do their best to argue against their own points of view to see if their views can withstand opposition. The writing of history is a brave business because good historians are willing to question all the evidence and all the assumptions, and in the end question themselves rigorously Throughout all historical inquiries, the relentless application of the journalistic questions will make you an active researcher and a historian of authority. Nothing is quite so destructive to a historian's reputation as to present conclusions that prove gullibility, laziness, or the unwillingness to ask questions that make the data provide real insight into the meaning of the past.

3

Modes of Historical Writing

Like other writers, historians use the four common modes of expression—description, narration, exposition, and argument. Of these, argument is nearly always the most important mode in the college classroom. Your instructor will require you to have a *thesis*, a point of view, a subject that unites your paper, a proposition you want others to believe. (*Thesis* comes from a Greek word meaning *to set down*.) That thesis will be the argument, the reason you write the paper, the case you want to prove. In the most basic meaning of the word, argument does not mean a dispute about something. The word originally meant *to prove* or *to assert*. At an earlier time people spoke of the "argument" of the novel, meaning the novel's plot and the view of human nature and possibility that informed the writer's way of presenting the story. So argument is rather a principle of organization that unites facts and observations to present a proposition important to the writer.

We should return to a fundamental point. A collection of facts is not an essay. The facts must be woven together in such a way that they support a well-defined point of view that the writer wishes other people to believe. If you take notes on your reading and assemble a vast collection of historical facts about Woodrow Wilson, you don't have an essay. But if you sift through your notes and discover that Wilson often expressed negative attitudes towards black Americans, you begin to have a thesis for an essay, something you want to examine under several heads. Why did Wilson have these attitudes? What did he do in response to them? What consequences did his attitudes and his actions have?

It may be that hardly any scholars have considered this aspect of Wilson's career. So when you write your own essay on the subject, you may not be arguing with anyone else. That is, you may not have a disputation, a debate with another historian on the subject. Still, your point of view is an argument.

A little later in this chapter we shall discuss argument as debate. But as we study the modes, we should recall that in writing history papers argument is the sense of a thesis, or a topic is fundamental to all the modes.

49

The modes overlap, and we may use all of them in a single paper. A narrative paragraph may tell how British troops ferried across the Back Bay of Boston on the night of April 18, 1775, were required to stand in a marsh in water up to their knees waiting for supplies they did not need before they tramped out to Lexington and Concord. A descriptive paragraph might give details of the marsh and the chill of an unusually cold New England spring. A brief exposition might consider the effects on tempers of having to march 12 or 15 miles to Lexington in cold, wet clothes and heavy wet boots. A writer might then argue that the needless delay in the Cambridge marsh robbed the British of the element of surprise and led to their humiliating defeat at the hands of the American minutemen in the battles that began the Revolutionary War.

Although the four modes often overlap, they are distinct, and one will usually predominate in a given book or essay. If you have a clear idea of the mode best suited to your purposes, you make the task easier for you and your readers.

DESCRIPTION

Description presents an account of sensory experience—the way things look, feel, taste, sound, and smell. Popular history includes vivid descriptions, and you can describe people and places with great effect in a paper intended for a college or scholarly audience. No matter how learned or unlearned we are in the limitless facts of a historical period, we have all had sensory experiences similar to those of people in the past. Our senses are the common denominator in human life. Perhaps as a consequence of our own reliance on sense experience, we like concrete details about physical reality in books and articles about history. Details reassure us that the world of the past was enough like our own world to let us imagine it, to place ourselves within it (for at least a moment), and to find it familiar and understandable.

Few historical papers are devoted to description alone—although an account of the geography of the Battle of Thermopylae might be largely devoted to a description of the Malliac Gulf and the narrow ledge or pass between it and Mount Callidromion. There, in August 480 B.C., three hundred Spartans stood off thousands of Persians until the Spartans died to the last man. Since then the hot sulphur springs of Thermopylae (the word means *hot gates* in Greek) have continued to flow, perhaps contributing to the silting up of the gulf, which has made the sea recede. On the site it is difficult to work out the exact geography of the battle. A paper on the topic might be carefully descriptive, providing the writer's reconstruction of these events and the geography that controlled them.

Never try to describe everything. You will suffocate your essay in details. Describe only enough to kindle the imaginations of readers. In his book *Sacco and Vanzetti: The Case Resolved,* part history and part autobiography, Francis Russell tells us how he changed his mind about the celebrated trial in 1921 and execution in 1927 of Nicola Sacco and Bartolemeo Vanzetti. The two were accused of murder in a payroll robbery that took place in South Braintree, Massachusetts, on April 15, 1920. They were tried in Dedham, Massachusetts. More than forty years ago Russell began his interest in the case by believing that they were innocent. After long and detailed study, he concluded that Sacco was guilty of murder and that Vanzetti was what in legal terminology is called an accessory after the fact, That is, Vanzetti knew Sacco was guilty but tried to help him escape the law.

The following descriptive passage sets the tone for the carefully reflective book that follows. It also has an implicit agenda intended to give readers confidence in the author of a controversial book, since received wisdom in the American liberal tradition held that Sacco and Vanzetti were innocent martyrs to Yankee New England's hatred of Italian immigrants.

> Someday, I promised myself, I was going to sit down and study the Sacco-Vanzetti trial transcript. But with the coming of the war, my interest lapsed. If I had not been called for a month's jury duty in the Dedham courthouse in the spring of 1953, I doubt that I should ever have concerned myself with the case again. I was then living in Wellesley, eight miles away, and when the weather was good I used to walk along the back roads to Dedham. By starting at quarter to eight, I could get to the courthouse just before ten o'clock, when the morning session began.
>
> I liked those brisk bright mornings, the earth smelling of spring, the maples in misty shades of mauve and red. From Wellesley the road dipped past the country club, curving down to Needham, a semi-suburb of repetitive three-bedroom houses, commonplace enough, yet—as I was later to discover—singularly interwoven with the Sacco-Vanzetti case.
>
> Spring was late that year. Not until my second week, as I crossed the bridge over the Charles River the other side of Needham, did I hear the creaky notes of the red-wings among last year's cattails. A few mornings later I saw a couple of painted turtles still torpid from hibernation. From the bridge I headed up the winding road to Dedham, past much empty land, orchards, stone walls, and the driveways of discreetly hidden river estates. Then, from Common Street on Dedham's outskirts, I swung

into High Street, ahead of me above the still-bare elms the courthouse dome, mosquelike in the early light, crowned by an ornate metal grille and a flagpole. On those placid mornings the flag hung limp.

It was almost a third of a century since Sacco and Vanzetti had been tried, yet the ghost of their trial still seemed to haunt the courthouse. Scarcely a day passed while I was on jury duty but some reference to it came up. It shadowed us all. We served in the same paneled room with the marble-faced clock where Sacco and Vanzetti had been tried and sentenced. There was the same enclosure for the prisoners that Sacco-Vanzetti partisans referred to as a "cage"—as if the two defendants had been exhibited like animals in a zoo. Actually, it was a waist-high metal lattice, slightly higher in the back, with nothing formidable or forbidding about it. Our white-haired sheriff, Samuel Capen, in his blue-serge cutaway, its gleaming brass buttons embossed with the state seal, and his white staff of office that he wielded like a benevolent shepherd, had been sheriff at the time of the great trial. In the overlong lunch hours he would sometimes talk about it, telling of the day Sacco and Vanzetti were sentenced, how Vanzetti made his famous speech, and how Judge Thayer sat with his head bent and never looked at him. I do not suppose any doubts had ever crossed the sheriff's mind as to the guilt of the two Italians or the rectitude of Massachusetts justice.[1]

Russell uses several forms of description. We have a direct appeal to the senses as when Russell tells us of colors ("misty shades of mauve and red"), objects ("the marble-faced clock"), sounds ("the creaky notes of the red-wings"), and smells ("the earth smelling of spring").

All these descriptions of physical reality depend on our having had some experience that he can summon up in our memories. When he tells us that the Dedham courthouse dome looked "mosquelike in the early light," he assumes that we know what a mosque is. We may not have had every experience he describes. Some readers may not have heard the "creaky notes" of red-wing blackbirds. Still these readers follow Russell's account because his description conveys authority; he has been there; he knows what he is talking about; his language conveys a familiar reality. These qualities help us believe him.

Another kind of description here is more impressionistic, more metaphorical. Russell tells us that the enclosure where prisoners sat in the courtroom had "nothing formidable or forbidding about it." He tells

[1]Francis Russell, *Sacco and Vanzetti: The Case Resolved* (New York: Harper & Row, 1986), 34–36.

us that the sheriff carried an official staff "that he wielded like a benevolent shepherd." These are his impressions. Someone else might have seen the "waist-high metal lattice, slightly higher in the back" as formidable and forbidding and might have judged that Sheriff Capen wielded his official staff like a warrior's club. Subtly, Russell has prepared us to believe his impressions because he has provided earlier vivid, benign, and believable details about his observations. He has created an "implied author"—dispassionate, warm-hearted, sharply observant, a writer we can trust. So we are prepared to believe him also when he passes to more subjective impressionist observations—the unthreatening quality of the prisoner's "cage," the benevolence of the sheriff's flourishing his staff of office. Description often combines these two elements—the concrete and the impressionistic. They work here to prepare us to follow the author into his much more controversial belief that despite the protests that swept America when Sacco and Vanzetti were put to death, the two men were guilty.

Never make things up when you describe something. Although some readers may be entertained by flights of fancy in historical writing, historians find them cheap and dishonest, and with good reason. Here are two paragraphs written by the late Paul Murray Kendall in his laudatory biography of Richard III, King of England between 1483 and 1485. They describe the battle of Barnet on the morning of April 14, 1471, in which Richard, then Duke of Gloucester, fought on the side of his older brother, Edward IV, against an effort by the Earl of Warwick to overthrow Edward.

> Suddenly there was a swirl in the mist to the left of and behind the enemy position. A shiver ran down the Lancastrian line. Exeter's men began to give way, stubbornly at first, then faster. Warwick's center must be crumbling. Richard signaled his trumpeters. The call to advance banners rang out. The weary young commander and his weary men surged forward. Then the enemy were in full flight, casting away their weapons as they ran.
>
> Out of the mist loomed the great sun banner of the House of York. A giant figure strode forward. Pushing his visor up, Richard saw that the King was smiling at him in brotherly pride. The right wing, driving westward across the Lancastrian rear, had linked up with Edward's center to bring the battle to an end. It was seven o'clock in the morning; the struggle had lasted almost three hours.[2]

[2]Paul Murray Kendall, *Richard the Third* (New York: Doubleday, 1965), 97.

Kendall's description evokes a vivid image of battle, but his scene is almost entirely made up. Our sources for the battle of Barnet are skimpy. We know that a mist lay over the ground and that the battle was confused. In the midst of the battle, someone on the Lancastrian side shouted "treason," and others took up the cry. The Lancastrian troops in the middle of the line, thinking one of their leaders on a flank had gone over to the enemy, broke and ran. Their leader, the Earl of Warwick, was killed while trying to catch his horse. But Kendall's description of Richard meeting his brother Edward is all fantasy. No wonder historian Charles Ross, in remarking on Kendall's account of Barnet, comments dryly, "The incautious reader might be forgiven for thinking that the author himself was present at the battle."[3]

Much worse than Ross's scorn is what such fictional details do to Kendall's credibility. His book aims at resurrecting the reputation of Richard III from Thomas More and Shakespeare who made him a lying hypocrite and a murderer, guilty of ordering the deaths of the little sons of Edward IV after Edward died. To believe such an argument against a predominant historical opinion, we must have confidence in our author. But a book so filled with fictional detail as Kendall's cannot be taken seriously by dispassionate and thoughtful readers, and it has been regularly ridiculed since its publication.

British historian John Keegan is much more circumspect in his description of the physical circumstances of the battle of Waterloo in 1815, where the British and the Prussians defeated Napoleon. Keegan has studied his sources carefully, and he can both report on what they tell him and infer other things from that information. Unlike Kendall, he tells us when he conjectures by using the word *probably;* his use of the sources makes us believe that when he says *probably,* he is probably right:

> Besides being hungry and travel-worn the combatants at Waterloo were also rain-sodden. The regiments that had spent the night marching lay down to sleep in wet clothes and probably woke up to fight the battle still very damp. Those which passed the nights in the fields, though they slept worse, or had no sleep at all, generally found means to dry out after sunrise. A young officer of the 32nd, who had woken wet through, managed to get into a shed where there was a fire and the men made large fires outside. The light company men of the 3rd Foot Guards, who had

[3]Charles Ross, *Richard III* (Berkeley and Los Angeles: University of California Press, 1983), 21.

spent the night "cramped sitting on the side of a wet ditch" south of Hougoumont, got a fire going "which served to dry our clothing and accoutrements," and Leeke, of the 52nd, found a fire large and hot enough to get some sleep by. Wood, of the 10th Hussars, an officer whose Waterloo letter breathes the authentic cavalry spirit, "got into a small cottage close to our bivouac . . . most of us naked, and getting our things dry at the fire . . . Old Quentin burned his boots and could not get them on." Other cavalry men, too, found their clothes spoiled by the wet. The Greys' scarlet jackets had run into their white belts overnight and Sergeant Coglan of the 18th Hussars attempted to dry his clothes by hanging them on the branches of trees. The Assembly was sounded before he had succeeded, and he dressed in the saddle, "crying out to those I had charge of to mount also." Waterloo day was overcast, rather than sunny, so those who, like Coglan, failed to get near a fire at the beginning presumably stayed damp until well after midday. Houssaye's "kaleidoscope of vivid hues and metallic flashes," his "bright green jackets . . . imperial blue collars . . . white breeches . . . breastplates of gold . . . blue coats faced with scarlet . . . red kurkas and blue plastrons . . . green dolmans embroidered with yellow braid, red pelisses edged with fur," must have covered many limp stocks, sticky shirts, and clammy socks.[4]

We can see here the common denominator of sense experience. We know what it is to have to go about in wet clothes, we recognize colors, and we know how hard it is to dry things in the open on an overcast day— or at least we know enough about wetness and overcast days to imagine that we know these things. I can imagine a soldier pulling wet clothes onto his body because on camping trips I have sometimes had to put on wet clothes in the morning, and I recall the miserable experience and sympathize with these men.

Keegan shows that description can give not only a sense of immediacy but can make us understand events better. His intent throughout the book is to answer this question: "How do men behave in battle?" His description of the men in the British and the French armies on the day of Waterloo fits into the rest of his book and helps us follow his argument.

NARRATIVE

Narratives tell stories, and stories are the bedrock of history. Without narratives, history would die as a discipline. Narratives tell us what happened, usually following the sequence of events as they happen, one

[4]John Keegan, *The Face of Battle* (New York: Penguin, 1984), 137.

event after the other—just as we tell a story about something that happened to us this morning.

Good narrative history often looks easy to write because it is easy to read. In fact, storytelling is a complicated art. As in description, part of the art lies in a sense of what to include and what to exclude, what to believe and what to reject. Narrative must also take into account contradictions in the evidence and either resolve them or admit frankly that they cannot be resolved. Who fired the first shot on the morning of April 19, 1775, when British regular soldiers clashed with the minutemen on the Lexington Green in Massachusetts? The incident makes a nice subject for narrative history—but it is not an easy story to write. Sylvanus Wood, one of the minutemen, dictated his account of the battle over fifty years after he fought in it under the command of Captain John Parker. Here is part of what he said:

> Parker led those of us who were equipped to the north end of Lexington Common, near the Bedford Road, and formed us in single file. I was stationed about in the centre of the company. While we were standing, I left my place and went from one end of the company to the other and counted every man who was paraded, and the whole number was thirty-eight and no more. . . .
>
> The British troops approached us rapidly in platoons with a general officer on horseback at their head. The officer came up to within about two rods of the centre of the company, where I stood, the first platoon being about three rods distant. They were halted. The officer then swung his sword, and said, "Lay down your arms, you damned rebels, or you are all dead men. Fire!" Some guns were fired by the British at us from the first platoon, but no person was killed or hurt, being probably charged only with powder.
>
> Just at this time, Captain Parker ordered every man to take care of himself. The company immediately dispersed; and while the company was dispersing and leaping over the wall, the second platoon of the British fired and killed some of our men. There was not a gun fired by any of Captain Parker's company, within my knowledge.[5]

Paul Revere had been captured by the British in the middle of the night before the skirmish. He told the British that 500 men would be waiting for them in Lexington. Lieutenant John Barker of the British Army was with the British regiment called the King's Own. He wrote an

[5]*The Spirit of Seventy-Six,* ed. Henry Steele Commager and Richard B. Morris (New York: Harper & Row, 1975), 82–83.

account of the battle only a few days afterwards, and here is part of what he said:

> About 5 miles on this side of a town called Lexington, which lay in our road, we heard there were some hundreds of people collected together intending to oppose us and stop our going on. At 5 o'clock we arrived there and saw a number of people, I believe between 2 and 300, formed in a common in the middle of the town. We still continued advancing, keeping prepared against an attack tho' without intending to attack them; but on our coming near them they fired one or two shots, upon which our men without any orders rushed in upon them, fired and put 'em to flight. Several of them were killed, we could not tell how many because they were got behind walls and into the woods. We had a man of the 10th Light Infantry wounded, nobody else hurt.[6]

How many American minutemen waited for the British on the green at Lexington that morning? The writer of a historical narrative must deal with the contradiction. You cannot pretend that the contradiction does not exist. Professor David Hackett Fischer, who has written the best book on the battles, did what you should do when you face such a contradiction. He looked for more sources, and he discovered a number of other depositions given by members of the Lexington militia and eyewitnesses. These investigations allowed him to make a sensible deduction: Many of the men the British soldiers saw as they advanced on Lexington were spectators, and some other minutemen joined Parker and his band after Sylvanus Wood counted the group. Here is part of Fischer's absorbing narrative. I have left out his numerous footnotes, but note his careful citation in the text of his sources:

> At the same moment the British officers were studying the militia on the Common in front of them. Paul Revere's warning of 500 men in arms echoed in their ears. As the officers peered through the dim gray light, the spectators to the right and left appeared to be militia too. Captain Parker's small handful of men multiplied in British eyes to hundreds of provincial soldiers. Pitcairn thought that he faced "near 200 of the rebels:" Barker reckoned the number at "between two and three hundred."
>
> On the other side, the New England men also inflated the size of the Regular force, which was magnified by the length of its marching formation on the narrow road. As the militia studied the long files of red-coated soldiers, some reckoned the force at between 1200 and 1500 men. In fact

[6]*The Spirit of Seventy-Six*, 70–71.

there were only about 238 of all ranks in Pitcairn's six companies, plus the mounted men of Mitchell's patrol, and a few supernumeraries.

The Lexington militia began to consult earnestly among themselves. Sylvanus Wood, a Woburn man who joined them, had made a quick count a few minutes earlier and found to his surprise that there were only thirty-eight militia in all. Others were falling into line, but altogether no more than sixty or seventy militia mustered on the Common, perhaps less. One turned to his captain and said, "There are so few of us it is folly to stand here."[7]

Fischer continues his absorbing story, working along the way to resolve the contradictions in his sources. By the time we get this far we have some understanding of why the British overestimated the patriot force. In a detailed appendix, Fischer tells us why he rejects Barker's number of "about 600" men in the British attacking force: Fischer went to the payroll rosters of the British army to see how many soldiers of the King's Own were collecting wages for their service. He recognized, as all historians must, that developing a narrative can be a complicated task. (After reading Fischer, I still think an argument may be made that Barker's number was correct, but that's another story.)

A good narrative begins by establishing some sort of tension, some kind of problem, that later development of the narrative should resolve. The beginning arouses our curiosity. We read on to see how it comes out. Children's stories demonstrate the qualities of any good narrative. We read, "Once upon a time a little girl named Cinderella lived in a house with her wicked stepmother and her two wicked stepsisters. Now the prince of the country gave a great ball, and he invited Cinderella's sisters, but poor Cinderella had to stay home and sweep out the ashes while her sisters went off to have a good time." We immediately know that Cinderella has troubles, that somehow the story is going to involve the sisters, the stepmother, the prince, and the ball. The story will reveal why all these details are introduced at the beginning.

A good narrative about history has the same qualities. It is not merely a recitation of facts. It introduces elements in tension and the rest of the story dwells on resolving or explaining that tension. Do not introduce material into your essay at the beginning if you don't intend to do something with it later on.

[7]David Hackett Fischer, *Paul Revere's Ride* (New York and Oxford: Oxford University Press, 1994), 188–189.

A narrative should have a climax that embodies the meaning the writer wants readers to take from the story. At the climax, everything comes together—the bill is passed, the battle is won or lost, the candidate is elected, the speech is made, the problem is solved or else explained. Because it gathers up all the threads and joins them to make the writer's point, the climax comes near the end of the paper. When you arrive at the climax, you are ready to wrap up your story, and your readers should feel that you have kept a promise made to them in the beginning. If you cannot think of a climax to your paper, you should reexamine your topic. If you cannot find a climactic point, you need to reorganize your story.

The story should move along, unburdened by unnecessary details. A good story can be enlivened by apt quotation. A principle of style worth remembering is that long block quotations may slow down a narrative. In telling a story, it is usually better to keep quotations short and pointed so that they clearly illustrate the events being recounted.

Here is a segment of narrative that explains how the Canadian force called the "North West Mounted Police" came into being. In the early 1870s, settlers on the plains of western Canada were plagued by lawless marauders from the United States and by frequent unrest in the Native American population. In a vast area called the "Great Lone Land" in Canada, no law enforcement existed. Sir John Macdonald, Canada's first prime minister (sometimes called "Old Tomorrow" for his habit of putting off decisions) decided to do something about it. Here is how writer Ogden Tanner carries on the story:

> At last, despite his habitual reluctance to move, Prime Minister Macdonald introduced an enabling act to the House of Commons. While drafting this legislation, he excised "Mounted Rifles" and substituted the wording "Mounted Police." Old Tomorrow in no way wanted to affront neighborly opinion below the border with anything that could be construed as Canadian militarism.
>
> The bill passed unopposed on May 23, 1873. Still in no great hurry, Macdonald planned to begin recruiting a force in the following year. But then an occurrence that took place almost simultaneously with the signing of the bill pushed him into what was, for him, precipitate action.
>
> In late May a band of American wolfers,[8] encamped a few miles north of Fort Benton in Montana, awoke one morning to find their horses gone. Reoutfitting in Benton, the "Thirteen Kit Carsons," as a

[8]wolf hunters

Montana newspaper later described them, set off northward to recover their stolen mounts.

A few days later, on a Saturday, the wolfers were encamped in a region north of the border known as the Cypress Hills. They were, fortuitously, located between two small whiskey traders' posts and, having the stuff handy, were toasting one another. The drinking went on all night and into the Sabbath. In the midst of their revels, they were joined by a Canadian named George Hammond, with whom they shared a certain community of interest. He, too, had lost a horse to Indian thieves but, by a stroke of fortune, had got it back from a friendly Assiniboine.

Now, on Sunday morning, Hammond went to check on his animal—and returned in a fury, shouting that it had been stolen again. The Canadian seized his repeating rifle and started for a nearby encampment of 40 Assiniboine lodges. The rest of the party, reinforced by six other Canadians, joined him. Later accounts held that the Indians, under a leader they called Little Soldier, were also drunk that morning. In any case, both sides started shooting.

The whites took cover in a gully, and Little Soldier's braves charged at them three times. One white man, a Canadian named Ed Grace, was killed as he rode up to join his companions. He was the only white casualty. But when the Indians finally withdrew and abandoned their camp, they left behind 30 dead.

The Cypress Hills Massacre, as the event was known throughout Canada, moved Alexander Morris, lieutenant governor of Manitoba and the North West Territories, to telegraph Ottawa: "What have you done as to Police Force? Their absence may lead to grave disaster."

The event galvanized Old Tomorrow into action. He ordered immediate enlistment and training of 300 men to be dispatched overland to Fort Garry before the freeze. And so one of the world's most respected constabularies, the North West Mounted Police, came into being.

Their scarlet tunic was an inspiration that had occurred to Adjutant General Patrick Robertson-Ross. Remembering that a green-uniformed Canadian regiment had moved Indian leaders to look dubious and say, "We know that the soldiers of our Great White Mother wear red coats and are our friends," he urged the Mounties to adopt red as their color. His reasoning was simple. "Animosity is rarely, if ever, felt towards the disciplined soldiers wearing Her Majesty's uniform in any portion of the British Empire," he said.[9]

This narrative begins with a tension to be resolved—the problem of lawlessness on the Canadian plains. It proceeds through the establish-

[9]Ogden Tanner, *The Canadians* (Alexandria, Virginia: Time-Life Books, 1977), 154–155.

ment of the North West Mounted Police. We realize when we get to the end that this is the goal towards which our writer has been leading us.

Pose these questions to yourself when you write a narrative:

A Writer's Checklist

✔ Why am I telling this story?

✔ Where do I want to begin?

✔ What happened?

✔ When did it happen?

✔ Who or what caused these things to happen?

✔ What details must I tell about these events, and what I can I leave out?

✔ Who were the major characters in the drama?

✔ What is the climax of the story?

✔ Where do I want to end?

✔ What does the story mean?

A narrative may be constructed from several sources, put together (as David Hackett Fischer does it) from many accounts given by eyewitnesses of the battle on both sides. But you may also construct a narrative based on one large source by extracting a story contained within it. For example, the great Canadian explorer, Simon Fraser, kept a journal in 1808 as he looked for a navigable river passage that he hoped would lead from central Canada to the Pacific Ocean. Had such a river existed, Canadians could have more easily transported furs from the Pacific coast to markets in the populous areas of Canada, and they might also have been able to lay claim to the territory that became the states of Washington and Oregon. Such a river did not exist. The river he found, ultimately named for him, runs into the Pacific considerably north of the Columbia River and the present border of Washington State, and it is not navigable through the mountains. His journal has been published, and it records his daring, his hopes, and his tribulations day by day. Using it as a principal source, a great narrative may be constructed. Collections of letters, as well as journals and collected papers, offer similar opportunities for narrative writing about other figures in the past.

EXPOSITIONS

Expositions explain and analyze—philosophical ideas, causes of events, the significance of decisions, the motives of participants, the working of an organization, the ideology of a political party. Any time you set out to explain cause and effect or the meaning of an event or an idea, you write in the expository mode.

As I have pointed out earlier in this chapter, exposition may coexist in an essay with other modes. The narrator who tells *what* happened usually devotes some paragraphs to telling *why* it happened—and so goes into expository writing. Some historical essays are fairly evenly balanced between narrative and exposition, telling both what happened and why, or else explaining the significance of the story. Many historical essays are primarily expositions, especially those that analyze, that break down a text or event to tell us what it means—even as they narrate what happened that makes the explanation necessary.

In college papers about history, exposition is usually the dominant mode. You may, for example, write an essay to answer this question: What did the founding fathers mean by the Second Amendment to the U.S. Constitution? That amendment reads, "A well-regulated militia, being necessary to the security of a free State, the right of the people to keep and bear arms, shall not be infringed." The essay you write in response would be an exposition. But it would probably include some narratives—the situation in 1789 when the Constitution was ratified, the situation today, the decisions of courts in the past on cases brought under the Second Amendment.

The study of the influence of one thinker on another or of one set of ideas on a historical process can make a good expository paper. You may even expound on the significance of some technological invention.

The view of human nature expressed in the *Federalist Papers*
A comparison between Thomas More's *Utopia* and Nicolo Machiavelli's
     The Prince
The significance of Woodrow Wilson's attitudes towards black Americans
Simon Fraser's attitude towards the United States
Quebec in the thought of Charles De Gaulle of France

All these subjects require analysis of texts, of events, or both. You must explain things, relate various texts to one another, make inferences, and perhaps ask some questions that no one can answer. When in a speech in Quebec City in July 1967, De Gaulle cried "Vive Québec Libre," was he pursuing a policy, or was he only trying once again to annoy the "Anglo-Saxons" whom he often treated with contempt because he thought they were contemptuous of France? It is hard to know. But the difficulty does not stop the historian from trying to answer the questions.

Here is an excerpt from one of the most famous books of the Renaissance, Baldessare Castiglione's *The Book of the Courtier:*

There are also other exercises which, although not immediately dependent upon arms, still have much in common therewith and demand much manly vigor; and chief among these is the hunt, it seems to me because it has a certain resemblance to war. It is a true pastime for great lords, it befits a Courtier, and one understands why it was so much practiced among the ancients. He should also know how to swim, jump, run, throw stones; for besides their usefulness in war, it is frequently necessary to show one's prowess in such things, whereby a good name is to be won, especially with the crowd (with whom one must reckon after all). Another noble exercise and most suitable for a man at court is the game of tennis which shows off the disposition of body, the quickness and litheness of every member, and all the qualities that are brought out by almost every other exercise. Nor do I deem vaulting on horseback to be less worthy, which, though it is tiring and difficult, serves more than anything else to make a man agile and dexterous; and besides its usefulness, if such agility is accompanied by grace, in my opinion it makes a finer show than any other. If, then, our Courtier is more than fairly expert in such exercises, I think he ought to put aside all others, such as vaulting on the ground, rope-walking, and the like, which smack of the juggler's trade and little befit a gentleman.[10]

Here is an exposition that uses this passage as part of a general treatment of the Renaissance. Insofar as possible, the expositor puts the thoughts of Castiglione into other words, words that may be more familiar and hence more understandable for readers today:

Baldessare Castiglione's *The Book of the Courtier,* the most frequently translated and printed book of the sixteenth century other than the Bible, presents itself as a dialogue on the qualities that make a good courtier. Courtiers, as the name implies, were members of a prince's court or entourage, helping him in various ways to rule his domain. In the sixteenth century, when Italy was divided among multitudes of city-states, princes needed talented men to help conduct

[10]Baldessare Castiglione, *The Book of the Courtier,* trans. Charles S. Singleton (Garden City, NY: Doubleday, 1959), 38–39.

finances, war, diplomacy, and other affairs. Without such servants and counselors, princes might lose power over a populace that was often fickle and rebellious.

Courtiers rose on their talents but also on their ability to get along with other people and impress their princes—not unlike the way people rise today in the corporate and political worlds. Castiglione's dialogue became not only an entertainment but also a handbook. Aspiring courtiers read it to learn how to conduct themselves as gentlemen and how to rise. It was the manners book of its day, popular alike with Spanish kings and English puritans.

Castiglione throughout writes on two levels. On one level the courtiers in his dialogue discuss ways of becoming more useful, better men. It is good to hunt, for example, for hunting calls for many of the same skills required in war. Evidently he refers to life in the open air, to riding on horseback in the chase, and to marksmanship—all helpful training for soldiers. Swimming, jumping, running, and throwing stones offer what we would call physical conditioning and provide basic training for war.

On another level Castiglione's characters are always concerned not only to better their skills but also to make a good impression. By performing feats of physical strength and agility, one wins a good name with the crowd "with whom one must reckon after all." Tennis with its leaping and quickness displays the body. Jumping on horseback both helps a man become "agile and dexterous" and "makes a finer show than any other." Some things make a bad show and are to be avoided no matter how useful they may be as bodily exercises. For some reason Castiglione cites "vaulting on the ground" as an act to be avoided, perhaps because that sort of leaping was a game of peasants who could not afford jumping horses. "Rope-walking," balancing oneself on a tight rope, is also scorned because it is one of the tricks of "jugglers," the traveling entertainers who put on shows for city crowds much as their spiritual descendants do today. Such entertainers were considered lower class and even slightly dishonorable.

Throughout his book, these two qualities come to the fore again and again—skill and reputation. The good courtier in Castiglione's mind possessed both. Thousands of readers pored over his pages to learn not only what they should be but also what they should seem not to be.

This exposition tries to make sense of a text from the past. Our world has greatly changed from Castiglione's—although some things remain similar. The exposition explains his ideas to us and defines terms, and provides a context for his thoughts. Castiglione used the common word *juggler*, which we might take to mean someone who tosses several balls in the air at once and catches them without dropping any of them. The older meaning of the term in both Castiglione's Italian and sixteenth-century English was a street entertainer, usually some sort of magician. By explaining this broader use of the term, the writer makes the expounded text more clear. Always define the essential terms of your exposition.

This exposition includes some inferences. The writer infers that juggling is forbidden to the courtier because it smacks of deceit, and courtiers are supposed to be honest. The writer infers that jumping or "vaulting" on the ground is forbidden because that sort of athletic activity is common to peasants who cannot afford horses. Peasants in Europe at this time were scorned by the educated classes who might be courtiers and who might read Castiglione's book. One cannot prove an inference, but inferences provide plausible explanations that may help fill out the meaning of a text. These inferences show a writer trying to make sense of things, and readers appreciate such thinking as long as it stays within the boundaries of the plausible.

ARGUMENT

Historians and others use argument to take a position on a controversial subject. It can be said that every essay contains an argument in that every essay is built around a proposition that the writer wants us to believe. Yet in common usage, an argument is part of a debate, a dialogue between opposing views—sometimes many opposing views. Arguments include exposition, for they must explain the writer's point of view. An argument also seeks to prove that other points of view are wrong.

Arguments are most interesting when the issues are important and all sides are fair to each other. The questions that create good arguments arise naturally as historians do research, weigh evidence, and make judgments that may not persuade others. Was Christianity, as Edward Gibbon held in the eighteenth century, a major cause for the decline and fall of the Roman Empire? Was Martin Luther a failure or a success? Did Al Smith lose the presidential election of 1928 to Herbert Hoover because Smith was a Catholic? Was slavery the main cause of the American Civil War? Have the poor of Cuba been better or worse off under the communist dictatorship of Fidel Castro than they were under Fulgencia Batista, the dictator Castro replaced?

The writing of history abounds with arguments about what happened and why. They arise because the evidence can be interpreted in different ways according to the assumptions of the historians themselves. Sometimes arguments continue until a consensus is gradually achieved. Did the German General Staff expect England to fight for Belgian neutrality if Germany invaded Belgium in 1914? For a long time many historians claimed that if England had declared itself clearly before fighting started, Germany would not have sent armies into Belgium, turning the conflict into a world war. But since the work of German historian Fritz Fischer, most historians have come around to the view that Germany planned all along to fight the English. Sometimes arguments rage for years, die down, smolder awhile, and flame up again. Did President Harry S. Truman drop atom bombs on Japan because he feared an invasion of the Japanese home islands by American troops would result in a million American casualties? Or did he know that the Japanese were already defeated and eager to surrender, and did he drop the bombs because he wanted to demonstrate the weapon to the dangerous Russians who, he recognized, would be the major foes to the United States after the war? The controversy over these questions raged for a time in the 1960s, died down, and now has risen again.

In any important historical issue, you will find disagreement among historians. The disagreements are valuable in that they keep us from becoming frozen in an intolerance of opposition, and debates may make us more tolerant in the present. The disagreements also help us see the sources in a different light. Disagreements thrive in book reviews. A historian who disagrees with another will make a counterargument to a book the reviewer thinks is incorrect. Jacob Burckhardt's *History of the Renaissance in Italy* published in 1860 has provoked a virtual library of response, books and articles arguing that he was right or wrong in his interpretation of the Renaissance—or arguing that he was partly right and partly wrong. Frederick Jackson Turner's frontier thesis has been similarly provocative.

The usual experience of the student of history is to study a great deal and to become convinced that someone else's argument is wrong or at least off the mark. Francis Russell's books on the Sacco and Vanzetti case represent this kind of discovery. The popular consensus among modern American historians was that Sacco and Vanzetti were innocent Italian immigrants hounded to their deaths by a vicious Yankee society for murders they did not commit. In 1955 Russell wrote an article supporting this point of view, published first in the *Antioch Review* and reprinted three years later with photographs in *American Heritage*. But as Russell continued to ponder the case, he slowly changed his mind. His publication of *Tragedy in Dedham* and *Sacco and Vanzetti: The Case Resolved* represents a crushing attack on the previous consensus.

Stay tuned to your own thoughts when you read sources. Where do arguments seem weak? Where do you feel uneasy about your own arguments? Can you see another conclusion in the evidence? Often good argument is a matter of common sense: Can we believe that something might have happened the way a writer tells us it happened? Many people who hated Franklin D. Roosevelt argued that he knew about the Japanese attack on Pearl Harbor in 1941 before it happened but kept it secret because he wanted the United States to go to war. Such a conspiracy would have involved dozens if not thousands of people—those who had broken the Japanese secret code for sending messages to the military and diplomats, those who monitored Japanese broadcasts, those who translated them and took the translations to the White House and the State Department, and the officials to whom they all reported. Is it plausible that such a vast conspiracy could have taken place without anyone ever stepping forward to talk about it, especially since any such report could have earned millions of dollars in book contracts? Our experience with human beings and their apparently uncontrollable yearning to tell secrets would seem to indicate that the answer to such a question would be no.

Good arguments are founded on skepticism. Come to history as a doubter. Study the evidence over and over. Read what other historians have said. See what the sources say. Listen to your own uneasiness. Do not take anything for granted. And when you decide to argue, be as careful—and as civil—as possible.

The Rules of Argument in Historical Writing

Here are some rules to help you make convincing arguments. Study them carefully and keep them in mind when you read the arguments of others.

1. Always state your argument quickly and concisely, as early as possible in your paper.

Get to the point in your first paragraph if possible. You will help yourself in making an argument if you state your premises early, shortly after telling us what your argument is going to be. *Premises* are assumptions on which your arguments are based. In writing about history, you may assume that some sources are reliable and some are not, and you will base your argument accordingly. You must then explain why you think one source is more reliable than another. Having done so, you can move towards your argument based on the premise of reliability.

All arguments are based on premises. Most Western historians take it for granted that Japanese militarism as it developed in the 1930s was disastrous for Japan and the world. But Japanese historians may assume that such militarism was the last effort to preserve a traditional society that had endured for a very long time, a society emphasizing collective rather than individual values, that the effort of the Japanese military was an unsuccessful but valiant effort to preserve the good of the past against Western imperialism. No matter how abhorrent such a position may seem to us, given the millions of deaths caused in Asia by Japanese aggression, the position makes us look at things in a different light, perhaps allowing us to see just how aggressive Britain, the United States, and other Western powers seemed to the Japanese at the time.

2. When you make an assertion essential to your case, provide some examples as evidence.

Journalists follow this principle almost always. A general statement is followed by a quotation or some other concrete reference to the evidence that provides support for the assertion. Readers need some reason to believe you. In writing about volunteer nursing by French women during World War I, historian Margaret H. Darrow deals with a paradox. The myths of war held that it was "full of honor, courage, heroism, self-sacrifice, and manliness." Nurses treating the wounded and the dying were caught not only by the power of the myth but also by the reality of what they saw; they had a hard time reconciling the two. Says Darrow:

> Few memoirs resolved the tension between the rhetoric of noble suffering and heroic sacrifice and the reality of dirt, pain, fear, and fatigue, with most memoirs swinging from one mode to the other without any attempt at reconciliation. For example, Noëlle Roger began her description of a ward of seriously wounded soldiers with the claim that "each of these men had lived a glorious adventure." She then depicted the shrieking pain of a man brought from the operating table, the rigid terror of a tetanus victim, and the hallucinations of a shell-shock case. However, her intent was not irony; she did not seem to notice—or could not express—that none of these were glorious adventures.[11]

Here is a standard pattern in historical writing—follow it whenever you can. The writer makes a general statement: "Few memoirs resolved the tensions between the rhetoric of noble suffering and heroic sacrifice and the reality of dirt, pain, fear, and fatigue, with most memoirs swinging from one mode to the other without any attempt at reconciliation." Then we get a quotation and a summary of the evidence. We believe the general statement because we have specific evidence for it.

3. Always give the fairest possible treatment to those against whom you may be arguing.

Never distort the work of someone who disagrees with your position. Such distortions are cowardly and unfair, and if you are found out, readers will reject you and your work, the good part along with the bad. Treat your adversaries as erring friends, not as foes to be slain, and you will always be more convincing to the great mass of readers who want writers to be fair and benign in argument. The most effective scholarly arguments are carried on courteously and without bitterness or anger. When you argue, remember the Biblical admonition of the Prophet Isaiah: "In quietness and confidence shall be your strength."

4. Always admit weakness in your argument and acknowledge those facts that opponents might raise against your position.

If you deny obvious truths about the subject of your argument, knowledgeable readers will see what you are doing and will lose confi-

---

[11]Margaret H. Darrow, "French Volunteer Nursing and the Myth of War Experience in World War I," *AHR* (February 1996):100.

dence in your sense of fairness. Most arguments have a weak point some-where. Otherwise there would be no argument. If you admit the places where your argument is weak and consider counterarguments fairly, giv-ing your reasons for rejecting them, you will build confidence in your judgments among readers.

Concession is vital in argument. You may concede that some evi-dence stands against your proposition. But you may then argue either that evidence is not as important or as trustworthy as the evidence you adduce for your point of view. Or you may argue that the contrary evi-dence has been misinterpreted. In either case you acknowledge that you know about the contrary facts, and you rob your foes of seeming to catch you in ignorance.

5. Stay on the subject throughout your essay so your argu-ment is not submerged in meaningless detail.

Inexperienced writers sometimes try to throw everything they know into an essay as if it were a soup and the more ingredients the better. They have worked hard to gather the information. They find their sources interesting. They want readers to see how much work they have done, how much they know. So they pad papers with much information irrelevant to the topic at hand. Sometimes they begin with pages and pages of background information and get into their argument only after they have bewildered readers with a story that does not need to be told. Get to your point. Trust your readers. Trust yourself. Make your argu-ments economical. Do as much as you can in as few words as possible.

Thinking about modes of writing will help you define more precisely the reason for your paper in history. Too frequently in history courses, students start writing without having any idea of the point they finally want to make about a topic. The instructor says, "Write a ten-page pa-per," and the student thinks only, "I must fill up ten pages." Well, you can fill up ten pages by copying the telephone book, but that won't be a good paper in a history course. Thinking about the modes will clarify your writ-ing task. It will also help your readers understand your purposes quickly. When I immediately understand what a writer is doing in a paper, my grade thermometer rises dramatically, and I become prepared to dis-pense high marks. Most instructors of my experience feel the same way. One of the hardest tasks an instructor faces is to have to read four or five pages into a paper before beginning to understand what the topic is. Help your hard-working instructor—and thereby help yourself—by writ-ing papers in which your command of the modes of writing will make your purposes clear.

Here are some questions to ask yourself about an argument you have advanced in an essay:

A Writer's Checklist

✔   Is this subject worth arguing about?

✔   Have I gathered enough evidence to make an argument?

✔   Do I represent the views of my opponents in a way they would consider fair?

✔   Have I developed my argument logically?

✔   Is my use of evidence accurate?

✔   Have I tried to prove too much?

4

Gathering Information and Writing Drafts

All writing is hard work if it is done well. Writing history has special problems—many of them discussed already in this book. But most people can learn to do it successfully—and thereby learn to do other writing well, too. The problems of gathering evidence, analyzing it, organizing it, and presenting it in a readable form are part of many writing tasks in the world of business, government, and the professions that include law, engineering, and others.

To start, you may need to rid yourself of some common myths. One is that writers are inspired, that real writers turn out articles and books and reports with the greatest of ease. Another is that if you must write several drafts of anything, you are not a good writer. Still another is that if you labor to get on paper what you want to say, you will not improve it much if you write a second or even a third draft.

Few writers manage to write without revising. The almost unanimous testimony of good writers in all disciplines is that writing is always difficult and that they must write several drafts to be satisfied with an essay or a book. The easier writing is to read, the harder it has been for the writer to produce it.

Your final draft must express a clear understanding of your own thoughts. But the way to that understanding may lead through several drafts. Writing, rereading, and revising clarifies your thoughts and strengthens your hold on your own idea. Once you have gone through that process, you have an essay that cannot be blown away by the first person who comes along with a firm opinion.

All writers use some sort of process—a series of steps that lead them from discovering a subject to writing a final draft. Different writers work according to different rituals. Eventually you will find your own way of doing things. In this chapter we shall walk through some common steps of writers on their way to books or essays. These suggestions may help you by showing how others write—but in the end you must develop the writing process that suits you best.

STEP 1: FIND A TOPIC

History papers begin with an assignment, usually expressed in the syllabus the instructor passes out at the beginning of the course. Read that assignment with great care. You will find in it the kind of topic your instructor wants you to write about, the evidence he or she wants you to use, and the length the paper should be. Follow those instructions carefully. The topic may be general within the limits of the course. "You will write a ten-page paper on a topic agreed on by you and the instructor." Or the topic may be explicit. "Write a ten-page paper on the reasons for the appeal of Lenin's 'April Theses' in 1917 during the Russian Revolution." In some courses you may write a historiographical paper. "John Reed, Richard Pipes, and Orlando Figes have all written books about the Russian Revolution. Write a ten-page paper exploring the differences in their attitudes towards the revolution itself."

Nowadays most assignments in history courses are general, and for most students finding the topic is an ordeal. Professional historians have the same problem. The ability to find your own topic reflects both how well you know the material and how you think about it. Defining your own topic is good discipline. A liberal arts education—including education in history—should teach you to ask questions and ponder meanings in every text you encounter in life.

Start with your own interests. You should be curious about people, events, documents, or problems considered in the course. This curiosity should make you pose some questions naturally. From the Russian Revolution of 1917 through the Vietnam War, Americans were obsessed with the dangers of Communism and the Soviet Union. But then the Soviet Union collapsed in a matter of months, something foreseen by no responsible person in American government. That amazing event should stimulate in all of us multitudes of questions that we ask to satisfy our curiosity about how such a thing could happen. The good historian is a questioner. As you read and attend class, you can help yourself by keeping a notebook in which you not only jot down notes about what you learn, but also the questions whose answers are not obvious. A notebook filled with questions will have lots of paper topics in it.

Never be afraid to consider a well-worn topic. Why did the Confederate army under Robert E. Lee lose at Gettysburg? What qualities of Christianity made it attractive to people in the Roman Empire during the first three centuries after Christ? What was humanism in the Renaissance? At first glance you may think that everything has been said that can be said. But when you look at the sources, you may discover that you have an insight that is new and different and worth exploring. The possibility is especially good if you study a few documents carefully and use them as windows to open onto the age or the event that produced them.

Sometimes you can find interesting topics in history by staying attuned to your own interests. If you are a religious person, you may naturally try to understand religious influences in the past. Do not use a history paper to convert someone to your own religious point of view. But religion is one of the most important continuing forces in world affairs, and it sometimes strikes me as odd that my students do not think to apply their religious interest to exploring how religion has influenced historical events. The same is true of interests such as sports, food, fashion, and other elements of life. I have often wondered when the French love affair with dogs began and what historical significance it may have. History is a much more open discipline than it once was, and with a little searching you may be able to translate one of your own consuming interests into a good research paper.

Here I must repeat an important axiom: Yours must be an *informed* interest. You have to know something before you write anything about history. Do not write an opinionated article off the top of your head. Good historians read, ask questions of their reading, read again, and try to get things right. It is typical of a historian to write with a pile of notes or a collection of notebooks beside the keyboard—or the yellow pad. Now it is becoming more and more common for historians to write with a well-stocked database stored in their computers.

Write Down Your Early Thoughts about the Material

Pianists do finger exercises before they play. Baseball players take batting practice before a game. These activities help them limber up for the real thing. Similar exercises will help you prepare to write.

After a lecture or a discussion in a section, write a brief summary of the important points made during the class and jot down all the questions that come to mind about what has been said. When you read, keep brief notes with page numbers on important information. You do not have to write extensive notes. The page numbers can help you find the information again when you need it. Write down questions about what you read. (I scribble copious notes and questions in the margins of all my own books. But NEVER, NEVER write in a library book!) I keep a separate notebook for each project I'm working on at a given time, using the blank books available now in most bookstores. You can carry a notebook in your backpack or book bag and whip it out to jot down ideas when they come to you. You can also use 3×5 cards or yellow pads or even a computer. Notebooks to me seem most convenient.

The main point is to jot down ideas and questions about several possible topics, unless one idea has struck you with such force that you know you will write about it. Many of these will overlap, but do not worry about that. The notes make you think, and in time one will dominate your attention. As you go on in this random, almost playful writing, several things may happen:

- You may become more aware of your own interests.
- You may define and refine your topic.
- You may start assembling and organizing evidence for your paper.
- You may start shaping the argument that you will make.

It's usually good to start writing soon after you get an assignment. Do not make this preliminary writing a rough draft. Simply set down your thoughts, perhaps in disconnected paragraphs that allow you to work out your ideas. You may write phrases or sentences without trying to work them into paragraphs. They will stir your mind to more thoughts.

Inexperienced writers often assume that an accomplished writer does all the research first and then writes. On the contrary, most experienced writers find that no matter how much they know about a subject at the start, the act of writing confronts them with new problems and new questions, gives them new leads, and sends them off in search of more information to pursue new leads, and even to come to conclusions different from those with which they began. For the experienced writer, the writing proceeds in a process of leaping forward and leaping back.

Different writers proceed in different ways. The process I have outlined here is typical for many if not most writers. But now and then we may grasp a topic so thoroughly after one round of careful research that all that remains is to set our notes out on the table and write a paper. That happy process is a rare event.

To postpone writing until one has done all the possible research on the subject can be disastrous. Many historians have fallen before the demand they put on themselves to read one more book or article before they could start writing. That was the fate of Frederick Jackson Turner, who, after propounding his "frontier thesis" of American history, was expected to write many important books. He signed several contracts with publishers without being able to produce the books. Historian Richard Hofstadter wrote the following sad words about Turner. They should be stamped on the skin of every historian tempted to put off writing:

> He became haunted by the suspicion, so clear to his biographer, that he was temperamentally "incapable of the sustained effort necessary to complete a major scholarly volume." "I hate to write," he blurted out to a student in later years, "it is almost impossible for me to do so." But it was a self-description arrived at after long and hard experience. In 1901 when he was forty, Turner had signed contracts for nine books, not one of which was ever to be written and only a few of which were even attempted, and his life was punctuated by an endless correspondence with disappointed publishers. For an academic family, the Turners lived expensively and entertained generously, and the income from any of the textbooks he promised to write would have been welcome, but the carrot of income was no more effective than the stick of duty and ambition. Turner's teaching load at Wisconsin was for a time cut down, in the hope that it would clear the way for his productive powers, but what it produced was only a misunderstanding with university trustees. Turner's reluctance to address himself to substantive history was so overwhelming that A. B. Hart, a martinet of an editor who presided with ruthless energy over the authors of the American Nation series, extracted *Rise of the New West* out of him only by dint of an extraordinary series of nagging letters and bullying telegrams. Hart in the end counted this his supreme editorial achievement. "It ought to be carved on my tombstone that I was the only man in the world that secured what might be called an adequate volume from Turner," he wrote to Max Farrand; and Farrand, one of Turner's closest friends who watched his agonized efforts to produce his last unfinished volume in the splendid setting provided by the Huntington Library, sadly concluded that he would not have finished it had he lived forever.
>
> Over the years Turner had built up a staggering variety of psychological and mechanical devices, familiar to all observers of academia, to stand between himself and the finished task. There was, for example, a kind of perfectionism, which sent him off looking for one more curious fact or decisive bit of evidence, and impelled the elaborate rewriting of drafts that had already been rewritten. There were the hopelessly opti-

mistic plans for what he would do in the next two or twelve or eighteen months, whose inevitable nonfulfillment brought new lapses into paralyzing despair. There was an undisciplined curiosity, an insatiable, restless interest in *everything,* without a correspondingly lively determination to consummate anything; a flitting from one subject to another, a yielding to the momentary pleasures of research as a way of getting further from the discipline of writing. ("I have a lot of fun exploring, getting lost and getting back, and telling my companions about it," he said, but "telling" here did not mean writing.) There was overresearch and overpreparation with the consequent inability to sort out the important from the trivial—a small mountain of notes, for example, gathered for a trifling projected children's book of 25,000 words on George Rogers Clark. There were, for all the unwritten books, thirty-four large file drawers bulging with notes on every aspect of American history. There were elaborate maps, drawn to correlate certain forces at work in American politics. There were scrapbooks, and hours spent filling them in. . . . There were, of course, long letters of explanation to publishers, and other letters setting forth new plans for books. There was indeed an entire set of letters to Henry Holt and Company, examining various possible titles for the last unfinishable volume—letters that the exasperated publishers finally cut off by suggesting that the matter might well wait until the book itself became a reality.[1]

Turner's life helps illustrate something I said earlier in this book. Writing history is brave business. At some point you have to settle down and do it, and doing it takes a kind of courage that every historian must summon up if he or she is to do the job.

STEP 2: LIMIT YOUR TOPIC

Our last paragraph brings us to an essential wisdom that every writer must learn. I have mentioned it already, but it needs to be repeated. In my experience the most common flaw in student papers is that the topics are so broad that the essays have no focus and cannot therefore develop an original idea based on the evidence. Keep these two points in mind:

---

[1]Richard Hofstadter, *The Progressive Historians* (New York: Knopf, 1968), 115–117.

- Your topic must be defined narrowly enough to allow you to write an interesting and informative essay within the limits imposed by your assignment.
- Your topic must be defined according to the sources available.

You cannot write an interesting and original paper entitled "Woodrow Wilson" or "Mackenzie King" or "Susan B. Anthony." In 2000 or even 6000 words, you can only do a summary of a person's life—suitable perhaps for an encyclopedia but not for a thoughtful essay that tries to argue a special point. Pick a limited issue with available texts or other evidence that you can study in depth and write about within the assigned space.

STEP 3: CONSIDER YOUR SOURCES

Make sure you have access to sources for the topic you want to write about, and use your library effectively. Students usually underestimate the sources available to them. A good prowl through your library as you look for a subject may reveal more than you dreamed. Reference librarians are my saints and heroes—professionals at finding things. Smart students and smart professors learn to talk to reference librarians about sources of information. Once when I was writing a carefully researched novel about going West in the year 1851, I asked a reference librarian at the University of Tennessee how someone might have amputated an injured arm on the Western plains at that time. In a wink she took me to a little book called *Gunn's Domestic Medicine* published in 1831. It provided complete and optimistic instructions. I had one of my characters follow those directions. Several doctors who have read the book since it was published have expressed cautious astonishment that I knew so much about amputating arms. Had I perhaps flunked out of medical school? No, I simply had a good reference librarian.

The Internet

The Internet, or the World Wide Web, is now a fact of life whose implications are staggering, and "net" and "web" have taken on meanings no one would have understood even ten years ago. It may be the most revolutionary mode of communication since the invention of radio, and some suggest it is the greatest leap forward since printing itself. Anybody with a worldwide web connection can set up a web page, and so web pages abound from individuals, from enthusiasts for this or that writer or painter or celebrity both living and dead. Naturally enough various fanaticisms abound in this uncontrolled electronic environment. If you want to post a web page and maintain that you were abducted by space aliens who introduced you to Abraham Lincoln in another galaxy, nothing can stop you. Given the variety of American society, you'll probably get a following who will tell you about their own conversations with Lincoln in outer space.

But many valuable and important resources are on the web, and they are growing. The university where I teach is completely "wired," as they say, and all my students have e-mail. Every night when I log on to our local network, I have mail from students, and quite often students from other universities write me—including many who use this book. (My address for any of you who want to use it is rmarius@fas.harvard.edu. Write; I shall respond.) When you read a book or article by a living historian, you may be able to reach that person by e-mail with a question and receive in return a generous reply.

Discussion groups of all sorts roar across the Internet every moment, and anyone with an interest in a particular subject or area can join most of these at no charge. In a discussion group people are online at the same time, and their comments roll across the screen in dialogue with one another. Discussion groups are bull sessions where people chat about Shakespeare or historical subjects or heaven knows what. Now and then something valuable gets said.

List servers (Listserv) are of more interest to research historians. Each list server comprises people interested in the topic to which the server is dedicated, and multitudes of these lists are of interest to historians. Members send messages that are in turn posted in the e-mail boxes of everyone on the list. Some lists are presided over by one or more directors who decide which messages will be posted. Others are free-for-all discussions where anything sent to the list is immediately sent to all the mailboxes in the group. You may find a list of descriptions of list servers at http://liszt.com.html.[2]

These lists offer the opportunity to ask questions about many subjects—books and articles, puzzles in evidence, current problems, anything at all relating to the interest group the list is intended to serve.

---

[2]The period at the end is not part of the address, so leave it out when you type an Internet address.

Each list has its own rules, including ways to join and ways to cut off your subscription. I belong to only one listserv, FICINO, devoted to discussion of topics in the Renaissance. The danger of belonging to several is that your mailbox quickly fills up, and you get a lot of information you don't want or need. Still, such groups form valuable communities, and you can tap into them in various ways to eavesdrop on postings that may aid you in your research.

Beyond the listservs are the wider resources of the Internet, and these are legion. To access the Internet, you must have a web browser. Browsers, offered by Microsoft, Netscape, Quarterdeck, and other software firms, help organize the seemingly infinite resources for the Internet so you can find things. Browsers connect with a number of search engines—Excite, Yahoo, Infoseek, and others—that connect you with subjects on the web. These search engines allow you a blank space where you can type in keywords related to your inquiry. The engine will search for a while and present you with a list of "hits," as they are called, locations on the web where at least one of those keywords is in the title.

Problems abound right here. If, for example, you type in the word "Luther" in your search engine, the hits will include material on Martin Luther, the German religious reformer of the sixteenth century, several colleges that bear Luther's name, Martin Luther King, Jr., the civil rights leader of the 1950s and 1960s in the United States, and probably a dozen or so people named Luther Jones or Luther Smith who have produced web documents on the dangers of granulated sugar or on new cures for baldness. So when you use a search engine, think of keywords that will lead you most swiftly to the sources that you can use. If you type in "Martin Luther German Reformer," you will limit the number of hits you get to a manageable list that you can then sample as you please. You waste time if you enter such words as "Rome," "Renaissance," "Italy," "modern" or "printing" in your search engine.

The quickest and most effective searches are those in which you have an Internet address for a website and go directly to it when you enter the net on your computer. (As in all computer-related addresses, the address of a website must be entered exactly. Lowercase and capitals in the address must be entered precisely. One keystroke off, and you cannot get on.) Once you enter the address on the address line of your Internet connection, you can hit "enter" on your keyboard, and the website will come up. For instance, one of the most valuable websites for students in college history courses is the Hanover Historical Texts Project maintained by Hanover College in Hanover, Indiana. The address is http://history.hanover.edu/texts.html.

The Hanover Project aims at scanning both primary and secondary historical sources from eight broad areas—the United States; the Americas Outside the United States; Africa; Europe; the Middle East; India and South Asia; East Asia and Southeast Asia; Australia and Oceania. The Project began in 1995, and it develops almost week by week. Just now it is strongest in sources from Europe and the United States. The section on Europe is superb.

A few keystrokes will offer various epochs of European history, including "Medieval," and a click of the mouse there brings up several headings, including "courtly culture." A click on that choice brings up lists of primary and secondary sources including a friendly challenge by one Pierre de Mass in France in 1438 to a fellow knight to joust before the king on a day to be named. The provisions of the challenge ensure that the horses will be protected from injury. The winner of the joust was to receive as his prize the helmet of the loser and present it to his "lady."

The challenge is presented in a modern English translation and an older English version. And throughout the site, one can click on various words and bring up links to other information, including some beautiful illustrations from medieval manuscripts showing knights jousting and a knight being dressed by his squire in preparation for the joust. This latter illustration shows a table with various parts of armor lying on it. Click on any part of armor, and a glossary pops up to tell you what it is called and how it developed in the course of medieval times.

We can imagine all sorts of papers that might use some of this material. From John Keegan's book *The Face of Battle,* we know that at the battle of Agincourt in 1415, such heavy armor proved to be disastrous for the French knights who wore it. Once they were knocked off their horses or off their feet, they could not get up again, and the lightly armored English slaughtered them where they lay. An interesting paper might consider the connections between sport and war in the Middle Ages (or in our own times) and demonstrate the dangers inherent in the confusion of the two. Material, including the illustrations, downloaded from these various linked sources could go into the essay.

The Historical Archive at Mississippi State University also offers a superb collection of documents, essays, images, and related material in the field of history. Like the Hanover Project, the Mississippi State Archive is expanding to embrace every region of the world. Its address is http://msstate.edu/Archives/History/index.html.

One of the best sites I know is maintained by Professor Carl Smith, an urban historian at Northwestern University. The site is supported by Northwestern and the Chicago Historical Society, and it is devoted to the great Chicago fire of October 1871. Hundreds of pages are devoted to photographs, paintings, drawings, newspaper accounts, and scholarly essays on the fire and its influence in Chicago's history. Professor Smith's site is a sterling model for anyone who constructs a website for purposes of scholarship and preservation. Its address is http://www.chicagohs.org/fire.

It's worth remembering that collections of primary source materials from all areas of history abound in libraries, and the Internet is by no means a substitute for a ramble through the stacks. Still, the speed of the Internet, the wealth of illustrations and other graphic materials available, and the ability to move easily from link to link make it an exciting source that you should explore with proper caution.

New prospects abound. At this writing, Columbia University Press is considering publishing some scholarly "books" online rather than in conventional book form. If other university presses follow suit, the results will be incalculable. The New York Public Library has established a site for images and texts about blacks and their history and culture in America. Various journals are already online all over the world. I regularly read articles in the German news magazine *Der Spiegel* on the Internet, and other publications in many languages abound. Many newspapers, including *The New York Times,* are available on the Internet. The *Encyclopedia Britannica* is on the Internet for a monthly charge. (It is also on CD-ROM.) Standard works of literature, often useful to historians, are on the Internet. Shakespeare is there as are extensive Latin texts from the Roman and medieval worlds. Multitudes of novels and other books published in the nineteenth century are online.

Increasingly, scholarly works are to be found on the Internet, and some scholarly journals are developing their own web pages that show tables of contents and sometimes abstracts of articles. Libraries all over the world are putting catalogues of their holdings online, and your own school library may be one of these. You can use the Internet quickly to roam through the catalogues of great libraries, including the British Library in London (once part of the British Museum) and the Library of Congress which by law is given a copy of every book published in the United States. Such catalogues are excellent tools to help you see what has been published on a subject that interests you.

Use the web cautiously, and be skeptical about it. It is not yet a substitute for a good library. Try to check out the information you get there with sources you know to be reliable. Websites sponsored by universities for various disciplines including history offer a great deal of credibility. University websites end with the suffix ".edu." Government websites, also fairly reliable, end in ".gov." Commercial sites end in ".com." Websites are changing all the time, and almost any list may soon be obsolete. I am indebted to Professor Nancy Gabin of Purdue University for most of the following website addresses that offer excellent possibilities for students in history.

http://www.history.hanover.edu/texts.html
http://www.msstate.edu/Archives/History/index.html
http://www.lib.byu.edu/~rdh/wwi
http://www.ashp.cuny.edu/
http://leo.vsla.edu/lva/lva.html
http://icg.harvard.edu/~hst1651/
http://www.loc.gov/
http://www.digital.nypl.org
http://www.chicagohs.org/fire
Note that most of these websites are in universities.

CD-ROM

CD-ROM is a technology for the mass storage of data and its quick retrieval by devices that use plastic compact discs that have long been used for recording music. At this writing CD-ROM technology is rapidly replacing the older magnetic diskettes that were essential to the microcomputer revolution that swept the United States and the world in the early 1980s. But in the wings is another technology using discs called DVM that may in turn rapidly displace CD-ROM.

For the moment CD-ROM has opened huge resources for the historian, and libraries great and small have installed the technology that makes data stored on CD-ROM easily accessible to users. Each time I walk into my own university's library system, I am startled to see that yet another CD-ROM resource has been added. By the time this book is published, doubtless more will be available. Here again you should consult your reference librarian. Reference librarians can direct you instantly to CD-ROM resources and can give advice on those most likely to be useful in your particular topic of research. Here are a few that I find indispensable. Remember that before a work appeared on CD-ROM, it was issued in bound volumes, and a good reference library will have these volumes going back to the beginning of the publication.

Historical Abstracts, published each year for many decades, has been on
    CD-ROM since 1981. Here are thousands of abstracts of books and

articles indexed according to author, subject, period, and place. You can browse the abstracts and see if the book or article pertains to your topic.

Lexis/Nexis consists of indexes to newspapers, periodicals, and court decisions.

The Social Sciences Citation Index covers hundreds of journals published in the social sciences since 1981. One can find articles according to subject, author, and title, and one can also find an index to all the footnotes used in the articles.

The Arts and Humanities Citation Index does what *The Social Sciences Citation Index* does but for the arts and humanities. It has indexed journals since 1974. Do you want to see how a novel or a book about the arts was reviewed when it appeared? You can readily discover the information in *The Arts and Humanities Citation Index.*

America: History and Life, updated annually, includes article abstracts and citations, an index to book reviews in American history, and an American history bibliography. It goes back to 1964, and it is a fabulous resource.

Most libraries now have a list of the CD-ROM resources available to users. Ask your reference librarian to give you such a list and to help you learn how to use the CD-ROM devices in your library.

Dissertation abstracts may be available. To obtain a doctorate in history, one must write a dissertation, an original, book-length manuscript dealing with a limited topic. Most dissertations are not published, but they contain tremendous quantities of information. Dissertations are increasingly placed on microfilm, and even if they are not, you can sometimes obtain them on interlibrary loan, although some schools don't allow their dissertations to be circulated.

CD-ROM is also becoming a splendid resource to preserve large works often consulted by historians. For example, the *Patrologiae Latina* is a collection of 221 volumes that preserve a vast chunk of medieval literature relating to Christianity from about 200 A.D. to about 1216 A.D. It is all in Latin, as the title indicates, and the volumes are huge. Now the whole set is on four CD-ROM discs. The search function on the CD-ROM makes it possible to do comparative research on subjects across centuries of time with remarkable ease. In working for the *Yale Edition of the Complete Works of St. Thomas More,* I once spent over two weeks looking for a quotation Thomas More made from a work he said was by

St. Cyprian, who died as a martyr in 250. It turned out that More was wrong, that the work he quoted from Cyprian was in fact written by a twelfth-century French monk. Later monks copying the work attributed it to Cyprian. Using the search function on CD-ROM, I could have found the reference in about a half hour.

Bibliographies

The bibliographical information on CD-ROM is increasingly important in helping you locate secondary sources about the topics you may write about in a history course. But not all bibliographies are on CD-ROM yet. Be sure you consult the *American Historical Association Guide to Historical Literature*, third edition, edited by Mary Beth Nortan and Pamela Gerardi, New York, Oxford University Press, 1995, in two large and heavy volumes. Here is a rich mine of information about books and articles on every aspect of world history.

In the same section of your reference room, you will doubtless find other bibliographies that will list books and articles, usually with something about their contents, on every conceivable subject.

Always compile a bibliography while you do research. Start early, and you will save yourself much grief. You can jot down titles in a notebook or on 3×5 cards. If you begin in the reference room of your library, note the full bibliographic references both to articles you read and to recommendations for further reading in the bibliographies appended to these articles. Look up your subject and related subjects in your library catalogue. Consult books and articles that include bibliographies and notes. Most online catalogues now have a function to look up books and articles not only on authors and titles, but also on subjects. Be sure to survey the journals in the field you write about. Go to the periodical room in your library and browse. Periodical rooms are pleasant places, and browsing gives you some insight into just how many specialized journals exist in the field of history and in other disciplines as well.

Students beginning work in history must learn that hundreds and perhaps thousands of scholars have written about topics that student writers choose to explore. Bibliographies, historical abstracts, and dissertation abstracts can help you as you write your paper. But they can also help you shape a topic for your paper.

To see how to cite both the Internet and CD-ROM discs, see Chapter 6 in this book.

STEP 4: DO RESEARCH

When you do research, take several steps:

- Consult sources.
- Formulate a thesis that helps you interpret these sources.
- Weigh the sources to decide which are most important to your purpose. That is, look at the sources critically to see what evidence they may contain to support or to contradict your thesis.
- Organize the evidence to tell as accurately as possible the story you want to tell.
- Put a design on the information so that it makes an essay.
- Cite the sources to let readers know where you have gotten your information.

Remember my earlier advice. Given the linear way in which I have described the steps in research, you may suppose that historians invariably follow these steps neatly one after the other. Not so! In practice things seldom run so smoothly. Historians may begin with one topic, discover another when they do research, and change their minds again when they start writing. As they write, they may redefine their topic, and as they redefine the topic they do more research. Writing our thoughts down often reveals gaps in our knowledge. So we go back to our research to fill in these gaps.

Start in the Reference Room

Start your research in the reference room of your library. Follow the advice in Chapter 2 of this book, "Thinking about History." Read encyclopedia articles and other reference books to get a broad overview of the topic. And don't forget that old reference books are valuable for providing widely held beliefs about topics when those books were published.

If you look up the same subject in many different reference works, many essential facts about your topic will be stamped in your memory. If in an American history course you decide that you might like to do a paper on President Woodrow Wilson, read five or six encyclopedia articles about him, some from old editions and others from more recent editions published after his death. You will then have different perspectives on his career as well as background knowledge of many events in his life.

Your reference room will have standard general encyclopedias—the multivolume sets such as *Britannica, Americana,* and *Collier's,* and single-volume encyclopedias such as *The New Columbia Encyclopedia* (my favorite), and the *Random House Encyclopedia*. Look also into reference works that may be specifically addressed to your field of inquiry. If you choose a topic related to religion, you might consult *The New Catholic Encyclopedia* in 15 volumes which contains a treasury of information on religious figures and religious movements of all sorts. *The New Standard Jewish Encyclopedia* provides a similar source for the history of the Jewish people and Judaism. All these articles will have brief bibliographies at the end listing standard works where you can find more information on a subject. It is enlightening to compare the article on Luther in the *New Catholic Encyclopedia* and then to look Luther up in the *New Standard Jewish Encyclopedia,* and yet again in the *Oxford Encyclopedia of the Reformation.*

The *International Encyclopedia of the Social Sciences* in 19 volumes provides information on issues interesting to social historians. The *Social Science Encyclopedia,* published in one thick volume in 1985 and edited by Adam and Jessica Kuper, is a mine of recent scholarship on social studies. *The Funk and Wagnalls Standard Dictionary of Folklore, Mythology, and Legend* in two volumes will give you information about folk beliefs in many societies both now and in the past. Sir James George Frazier's multivolume masterpiece, *The Golden Bough,* is a treasury of mythological lore combined with astute anthropological insights. *The Encyclopedia of World Art* in 15 volumes is filled with information about art and artists, and the recently published *The New Dictionary of Art* in 34 volumes by Grove Press is an even more stupendous collection of material on the same subject. *The New Grove Dictionary of Music* in 20 volumes does much the same thing with music of all sorts.

The multivolume *Cambridge Ancient History, The New Cambridge Mediaeval History,* and *The New Cambridge Modern History* are filled with authoritative articles, sometimes written without much verve but still worthwhile. *The Harvard Guide to American History* in two volumes is useful. The *Dictionary of National Biography* is indispensable for any work on British history. *The Dictionary of American Biography* is much inferior, but one can find there interesting information about important Americans who may be subjects of historical research. Many librarians have old nineteenth-century biographical encyclopedias, and these are not to be scorned although the articles are nearly always laudatory, and it seems as if the people—nearly all of them men—paid in some way to have their names included, perhaps by buying the books.

Government documents are invaluable resources. Federal, state, and local governments issue publications on innumerable subjects. The federal government has designated many libraries as repositories. That is, everything the federal government publishes is deposited in those libraries. The indexes are good and easy to use. You can find census information that is priceless in the study of history, reports on matters as diverse as the assassination of President John F. Kennedy to government recommendations for proper nutrition. Many libraries that are not official repositories subscribe to the *Congressional Record* that records everything said on the floor of the House and the Senate of the United States. (One must be cautious in using the *Congressional Record,* for Senators and Representatives have the right to read into the *Record* things they have not really said in speeches on the floor.)

Do not hesitate to use reference works in foreign languages. Even if you don't read the language or don't read it well, you may discover illustrations or other useful materials. If you have had a year or two of study in the language, you may discover that you can read the articles far better than you suspected. That discovery may draw you into further use of it—an advantage to the student of history. Knowledge of a foreign language is essential to advanced work in most historical fields.

Now let's consider these steps one at a time.

Primary Sources: Editions of Complete and Selected Works

Be on the lookout for editions of the works by the various people who may enter your paper. Using texts written by those you write about gives your own work authority. When you use any edition of collected or selected works, check the dates of publication. Sometimes several different editions have been published of the same works. Usually, but not always, the best editions are the latest. These editions may be of different sorts. The most valuable are editions of the complete works in which every surviving text is collected and indexed, sometimes with other materials from the time the person lived.

The essential source for a paper on Woodrow Wilson would be the great Princeton edition of his complete papers edited by Arthur S. Link and others. Use the indexes in such editions. If you become interested in Wilson's attitudes towards black Americans, look in the index to see both where blacks are mentioned in general and which particular black leaders are named. (In the Princeton edition of Wilson's works, entries for black Americans are found under the heading "Negroes.") The papers of presidential confidants and government servants are often published. The papers of Edward Mandell House, long a confidant of President Wilson, have been published. Political papers of many sorts in various foreign countries may be published, and you should examine your library's catalogue to see if any of these editions are available.

David Lloyd George, Prime Minister of Great Britain at the end of World War I, published a two-volume autobiography in which he spoke frequently—and critically—of Wilson. If you write about the attitude towards Wilson of various heads of state with whom he worked, consult Lloyd George's work. As your knowledge of people around Wilson enlarges, you can consult the library or bibliographies in encyclopedia articles about these people to see what books they wrote.

Complete works of various writers and historical figures are also widely available. The works of Benjamin Franklin, James Boswell, and Thomas More have been rolling out of Yale University Press for decades. (The More edition has just been completed.) Almost every large university press is involved in somebody's complete works. These editions come with copious notes and scholarly introductions.

Editions of correspondence are also common. Most of us love to read letters because, like photographs, they give us a sense of intimacy with bygone times and people we have not known. Like photographs, letters are quickly datable. One quickly sees that they belong to a certain time and place, and in the eternal flux of things, they seem to make time stand still for a moment. Collections of correspondence give us figures in relatively unguarded prose, commenting on daily life without the caution that marks more public utterances. The private persona or personality of the letter writer may be different from the public image displayed in speeches or writing intended for a large audience. Letters may also provide information not available elsewhere. Published diaries are often available. I have mentioned already the letters and diaries of the English writer Virginia Woolf, which opened a window onto her English world at the time of World War I and afterwards. If your library has a manuscript collection, you may find unpublished diaries and letters to help fit the pieces of your topic together.

Read autobiographies, but be skeptical of them, and check them against other sources when you can. When we write anything about ourselves, we have a natural desire to put ourselves in the best possible light for posterity. Autobiographies almost always have a lot of fiction in them. Still, autobiographies exist, and all of them contain some truth—although some are more truthful than others.

Other editions of various sources relating to a general topic are also collected and published. One of the most monumental of these collections is *The War of the Rebellion: A Compilation of the Official Records of the Union and Confederate Armies,* published in 70 volumes and containing, it seems, a transcription of almost every scrap of paper exchanged within the armies on both sides in the Civil War. (The noise of battle during the Civil War was so tremendous that men under fire could not hear each other speak. Therefore written orders carried from place to place on the battlefield were much more common than in earlier wars, and thousands of these were collected by the editors.) *The Calendar of State Papers, Spanish* includes English translations of all the letters exchanged between the Spanish ambassadors in London and their sovereigns at home during much of the sixteenth century, and so constitutes an edition of documents, not all by the same author. Generations of historians have used *Documents Illustrative of English Church History,* edited by Henry Gee and William John Hardy in one large volume and published in 1921.

These and many others that could be listed are examples of collections that can help you in research. Whatever your topic, check to see if your library has a collection of published documents related to your paper. Browse through such collections even if you don't at first see that they are related to your topic. You may be pleasantly surprised. Some topic can catch your eye, and suddenly you are on your way.

Secondary Sources

The bibliographies in the articles you read in reference works will give you a start towards both the primary and secondary sources for your study. The secondary sources will broaden your understanding and help you see the problems and opportunities in the sources as other writers have seen them.

Books.   Secondary sources will be of two general sorts—books and articles. A few bibliographies are annotated. That is, the compiler offers a brief comment on the books and articles he or she has noted:

Contamine, Philippe, *War in the Middle Ages,* trans. Michael Jones (New York: Basil Blackwell, 1986.) A lively account of how wars were fought from the barbarian age to the Renaissance. Includes not only an analysis of tactics and strategy but also discusses various theological and ethical attitudes towards war. Illustrated with both photographs and diagrams.

An annotated bibliography may be unreliable; the writer may judge some books too harshly, some too generously. But such a bibliography usually provides worthwhile information about the contents of books and articles.

You can often locate books about your subject more quickly than you can find articles. The reason is simple; the titles of books show up in the catalogue of your library and articles don't. (Thanks to computer indexing, articles are much easier to locate than they once were; in the next section, I'll tell you how to find them.)

The card catalogue in your library will list books under subject headings and by author. Under "Wilson, Woodrow," you will find biographies of Wilson and other books with Wilson as a major subject as well as books Wilson wrote himself. The alphabetical listing of books by their authors may list several titles by the same scholar. Because historians tend to specialize, several books by one author may be related to your inquiry. Another excellent way to locate books is to go into the library stacks and look at the volumes classified in one section. Many books about Woodrow Wilson will be on the same shelf. The footnotes or endnotes of books and articles can serve as references to other scholarly works about your subject.

Don't limit yourself to books about Woodrow Wilson; look for books that deal with his times. You may consult books about World War I, books about the progressive era that he represented, books about people close to Wilson, and about various issues in which he was involved. In such works you would look up the name, "Wilson, Woodrow" in the index and turn to those pages to see how Wilson is mentioned. You might discover yourself on the trail of a valuable insight.

Articles.   Hundreds of periodicals deal with history. Some publish articles about particular facets of history—the Middle Ages, military affairs, science, art, etc. Some have a scope as wide as the discipline itself. An afternoon spent consulting the annual indexes of bound periodicals can open your eyes to many issues that touch on your subject. New interpretations and information about any discipline usually get into print first in articles. To stay on top of a field, you must consult the periodical literature, the literature in journals.

Academic titles usually are fairly straightforward—often a catchy phrase followed by a colon and an explanatory subtitle. When you consult an index, you can quickly find articles of interest. Your library will keep an index for all the periodicals it takes, usually online and available at the same computer terminals where you will find other holdings in your library system.

Here are a few historical journals you might wish to consult. The list is by no means complete. I include it only to provide a start in your own efforts. Looking at these journals will help you see how vast periodical literature can be. Since the essays you write in a history course are more like journal articles than books, the journals will provide models of writing and thinking that you can imitate.

Your reference room will have *The American Historical Review,* the journal published by the American Historical Association to which most professors of history belong. Don't be misled by the title of the periodical; it is not limited to topics about American history. The *AHR*, as the title is usually abbreviated, carries articles about all aspects of history in all the regions of the world. The journal *Past and Present* publishes many diverse articles about history. *The English Historical Review* includes articles from the entire range of history, and one is likely to see an essay on early modern China just before another on nineteenth-century America. The *Historical Journal,* also published in England, strives for a similar breadth. The *Journal of Modern History* does not carry articles about the period before 1500, and most of its authors consider topics from the eighteenth century to the recent past.

Regional journals abound. *The Journal of the West* is specialized, carrying articles dealing with the history of that part of the United States that lies west of the Mississippi River. Another regional periodical is *The Journal of Southern History,* which treats the Southeastern United States, the region of the old Confederacy. *The Tennessee Historical Quarterly* will narrow the field even further, treating topics dealing with the state of Tennessee. Every state in the United States has at least one journal devoted to its own history, and many large cities have historical societies that publish a regular journal or occasional monographs.

The Journal of American Culture is specialized in a different way; there you are likely to read about popular culture, and you may see articles on TV commercials and on the history of comic books. *Church History* is specialized in still another way, featuring scholarly articles about the history of Christianity around the world. *The Catholic Historical Re-*

view includes articles about the same field, and despite its title often carries essays about Protestants and Protestant theology.

Finding Relevant Articles

These titles represent only a tiny percentage of journals published in history. In this mass of publication, how do you find the articles that may pertain to your subject? I have advised looking for sources in the notes and bibliographies of books that have been written about your topic. Outstanding articles get read and quoted and appraised by other scholars. Pay attention to footnotes or endnotes where a writer mentions the literature related to the subject. I mentioned earlier that searching the annual indexes of historical periodicals is an excellent way to find articles on your topic. While searching for articles on Luther's ideas about justification by faith in the indexes of *The Journal of Modern History*, you may run across Jean Wirth's review article of 1985 in which he surveys the major works on Luther published to commemorate the five-hundredth anniversary of the birth of the German reformer in 1483. Wirth's wisdom, wit, and comprehensiveness will give you an insight into modern Luther scholarship that you might not have seen otherwise.

Book reviews in historical journals provide another valuable source of bibliographical information. Most journals publish reviews, usually in the back of the issue. These are written by specialists in the various fields. Journals may classify the books reviewed by historical period or by subject. You can easily locate the books published about the time period that interests you most.

Reviews vary widely in their value; some are impressionistic, some bad tempered and malicious, some far too gentle or laudatory, some cursory summaries. But a review by a widely published expert in the field may provide a good appraisal of the strengths and weaknesses of the book—although sometimes experts have a tin ear to radically new and important developments in their fields. Very often a good reviewer will mention another book or article relating to the theme of the book immediately under review. By reading reviews you can pick up information about the field itself that you might otherwise miss, and you can find bibliographical references that will help you find books and articles relevant to your topic. If you read seven or eight reviews of the same book, you will get a pretty good idea of how specialists in the field regard it.

Of great value are the indexes to periodical literature to be found in all good libraries. The most common of these and the best known is *The Reader's Guide to Periodical Literature* which has been regularly published since 1900. Updates appear throughout the year, and at the end of each year a large, comprehensive edition is published. *The Reader's Guide* surveys only magazines intended for a general audience. Don't scorn this purpose, for you may find interesting, well-written articles by important specialists by consulting *The Reader's Guide.* You will not find articles published in the specialized journals and intended for professional historians, articles most likely to provide the information and the interpretations you need in a paper intended for a history class.

Fortunately the computer has come to the rescue. *The Permuterm Subject Index* and *Citation Index* for the arts and humanities and for the social sciences are now essential tools for every working historian. The indexes are issued annually on CD-ROM and updated half way through each year. Here one may find the name of every author who has published an article in any one of hundreds of specialized journals surveyed by the editors. One may find a listing of every significant word that has appeared in every title of the articles surveyed, these words arranged so that one may rapidly locate articles related to one's own field of inquiry. If you were looking up material on Woodrow Wilson, these indexes would include the title of every article that included the words "Woodrow Wilson." If you were looking up material on the Great Depression of the 1930s, these indexes would include every title that included the word "Depression." Full bibliographical information is given for each article, and every source mentioned in the footnotes or endnotes of the article is also listed. The result is a splendidly usable guide that will allow you to find quickly and easily the latest scholarly articles on the subject you are pursuing. If you have trouble getting the hang of it, your reference librarian can help you.

Almost as spectacular is the computer index called *American History and Life* published annually in three volumes, one with article abstracts and citations, one an index to book reviews in American history, and the third an American history bibliography. Abstracts are valuable wherever you find them; they summarize the argument of an article, leaving you the option to seek the article out and read it for yourself. These computer index publications don't as yet include articles published before computer indexing began in the early 1980s. But compilation of computer-indexed bibliographies in various fields has become an academic industry, changing and growing constantly.

Various firms are putting older material on computer software, especially CD-ROM, with as much zeal as publishing businesses in the 1950s and 1960s put old books and newspapers on microfilm. Your reference librarian can help you locate firms that will provide a computer-generated bibliography for almost any subject. Prices and quality vary, but the technology is improving all the time, and this sort of bibliographical aid has become a common and indispensable tool for historical researchers.

Book Reviews

Book reviews are a special form of writing that students often fail to appreciate. They provide a valuable source of bibliographic information. Most historical journals publish reviews, usually in the back of the issue. The most comprehensive coverage of reviews of books about history is to be found in *The American Historical Review*. But specialized journals exist for every area of historical interest, and almost all of them carry book reviews. These are written by specialists in the various fields, and it is an education in the state of historical knowledge at any given moment to read reviews.

Reviews are valuable for many reasons. They identify books and provide some idea of the contents. You can read a review to see if you should consult the book for information and interpretation of your topic. Book reviews may also introduce you to the field of discussion that surrounds any book that contributes to scholarship. A reviewer will tell you whether the book repeats old information, breaks new ground, contradicts received interpretations, and often whether the book is well written or else written in the style of some insurance policies, almost impossible to understand.

Reviews can be fiercely polemical, displaying historians at their worst. But then some books deserve to be attacked because they ignore scholarly evidence and present a one-sided view of their subject, often with a view of making a saint of someone who fell abysmally short of sanctity. More often uncivil reviews reveal pettiness and sometimes jealousy, and it is unfortunately often true that historians with radically new insights into a historical problem may be pummeled by old believers who think the truth was discovered long ago. Still I know of scarcely any better way to be introduced to the historical profession than by reading lots and lots of books reviews. You should by all means read as many reviews of the same book as you can since different scholars will highlight different aspects of a book. And you will often pick up information that you would otherwise miss.

Unpublished Materials

Most history papers are written from published sources. But don't dismiss other kinds of information. Many libraries include archives that house collections of unpublished papers of immense richness and variety. Why was a certain building constructed on your campus? Why was your college founded? Why did the founders locate it where they did? You may have to go to archives to find such information.

In my first teaching job, I spent two happy years at Gettysburg College, founded by the Lutheran Church of America in 1832. My department chair, Robert L. Bloom, asked himself why the Lutherans chose Gettysburg, and he went to the archives and came up with material for a delightful lecture. The center of the Lutheran Church in America has long been in Philadelphia, but in 1832 the Lutherans regarded this thriving port city as a sink of iniquity where pious students would be tempted by sins that sailors especially enjoyed. The Lutherans decided to establish their new college in Gettysburg, a quiet rural community where nothing important had ever happened, because they assumed that their students would be freed from temptation. Thirty-one years later, General Robert E. Lee arrived at Gettysburg unannounced with his Army of Northern Virginia where he was somewhat rudely greeted by General George Gordon Meade with his Army of the Potomac—men dressed in blue. The three-day battle fought at the edge of the beautiful college campus there apparently did not lead to the kinds of sin the founders had most feared, although ever afterwards no one could claim that nothing ever happened at Gettysburg.

Your own college probably has an archive, and if it does not, you can still find materials on how it was founded and why. Your library may have collections of unpublished letters, diaries, memos, and other materials. If you do a topic in American or Canadian history, take a look. There's nothing quite so thrilling as to look at the basic raw materials of history preserved in such sources.

Many libraries now include oral history collections, tapes, and records of people well known and obscure discussing the past and their participation in events then. You can sometimes learn something by the tone of voice people use to describe past events. A comparison between someone's oral recollections and written accounts can make an interesting topic for a paper.

Interviews are valuable for studies of recent or fairly recent history. If, for example, you write about some aspect of combat in World War II, you can find many veterans to tell you of their experiences, giving you a first-hand view of history. The same is true of the civil rights movement in the United States, the Vietnam War, the Great Depression, the Jewish Holocaust in Europe, and many other events within memory of witnesses and participants still alive. People who participated in great events are often eager to talk about them. Don't be afraid to call people up to ask for an interview.

Prepare for the interview by learning all you can about the person and by writing out questions beforehand. But don't be mechanically bound to your list before the interview begins. Explore each question thoroughly. Listen to your source and be prepared to ask for clarification of details.

The pleasures of all these methods of inquiry are immense. Historians who have worked in the archives or who have heard the actual voices of witnesses to history experience a satisfaction that can hardly be described. Reading one of Henry David Thoreau's essays in manuscript, and holding the paper that he held as he wrote are all special delights to the person writing about Thoreau.

To some it is even more moving to hold the letters or other papers written by men and women much more obscure, people forgotten except for some striking personal imprint of themselves left in writing. Both Yale University and the Huntington Library in California have large collections of diaries kept by people, especially by women, who went across the Western plains in covered wagons in the mid-nineteenth century. Sometimes the reader can see the stains left by a rain that fell over a century ago, and one can often tell something about the difficulty of the journey by noticing the changes in the handwriting. At some point every student of history, whether amateur or professional, should have the pleasure of looking at such a source.

The Reciprocal Interplay of Sources During Research

The relation between primary and secondary sources is complex. Many times in reading a book about a topic, something may arouse your curiosity, and you will consult a primary source to learn more about it. Or it may work the other way. Your reading of Shakespeare's play *Othello* will introduce you to the hateful villain Iago whose conspiracies cause Othello to murder his wife Desdemona in a fit of insane jealousy. The play is a primary source, and in the notes you will find that *Iago* is the Spanish word for *James* and that Saint James, *Santiago,* was the patron saint of Spain's fight against the Moors and that indeed Santiago was called *Matamoros,* killer of the Moors. Othello is a Moor, and Iago hates him. Spain was the most threatening enemy of England in Shakespeare's time. Off you go in search of secondary sources, books and articles, to see what the relations between Spain and England were when Shakespeare wrote this play. Was he trying to warn England of Spanish perfidy? You may have an interesting interdisciplinary essay stimulated from this literary primary source.

Taking Notes

Both the gathering of titles and your later reading of these books and articles will require you to take notes. Take scratch notes as you do your preliminary reading. Ask yourself questions, jot down significant phrases, and note places where historians disagree on the subject you are pursuing. Pay attention to what one historian notices that another ignores. One writer may write much about Luther's hostility to Jews; another may ignore the subject altogether. Why? Jot down your own opinions about both the historians and the material. Even in the early stages of your research important ideas may pop into your head. Write them down, and test them with further study. You may discover that further research confirms that some of your first impressions are gems.

Computers add facility to note taking. If you copy notes into a computer file, you can locate words by using the search function on your word processing program. Most programs will allow you to shift your notes to the file holding your essay when you begin to write. For larger projects such as an M.A. thesis or a Ph.D. dissertation, database programs offer even more variety in ways to preserve and retrieve your notes.

Review your notes at the end of each day. When you go over your notes, you sometimes begin to see connections that you don't make at first. By continually reviewing your notes you also impress them on your memory. Our short-term memory is flighty. You can read something, be intensely engaged in it, and take notes about it—but then forget it quickly if you don't do something to renew the experience. Reviewing notes fixes them in your mind and makes you remember them better so that you find them easily among your thoughts when you start to write. Reviewing your scratch notes will help you hold on to ideas that will then be nurtured by your subconscious powers of incubation, the almost miraculous ability of the mind to work while thinking of other things or even sleeping. Reading the notes over again will stir up thoughts that will contribute much to the final conception of your paper, and such reading will clarify the method you use to approach that goal.

The Forms of Notes.   Always include bibliographical references in your notes. For books, write down the name of the author, the title, the place of publication, the publisher, and the date of publication. For articles, include the name of the author, the title of the article within quotation marks, the title of the journal underlined or in italics, the volume number (if any), and the date (if any) and the year in which the article appears together with the page numbers of the article, and of course the page number of any direct quotation you copy from the article:

> Hyatt, Irwin T., *Our Ordered Lives Confess,* Cambridge, Mass., and
>
> London: Harvard University Press, 1976.

Later on you can refer in your notes simply to "Hyatt, 27" to locate your source of information. If you cite several books or articles by the same author, give the author and an abbreviated form of the title for your notes. Instead of giving the full bibliographic information for Woodrow Wilson's *History of the American People,* you can write, "Wilson, *History,* 4 (to indicate the fourth volume in the set), 160." Your main principle is this: Be sure you remember where you got your information. You must be able to refer accurately to your sources when you write. You will save yourself much grief if you keep track of them carefully while you do your research.

In addition to bibliographic references, take three other kinds of notes as you do research. The first is direct quotation. Always place direct quotations within quotation marks in your notes, and copy the quotation accurately. Make accurate reference to the page or pages of the source of the quotation. You may want to put a heading on the note to help you remember why you took it down. Always review the quotation for accuracy once you have written it down. The eye and the hand can slip while you are looking first at your source and then at your notebook, card, or computer screen. When you type, fingers can go astray, typing one word when you mean another. It may help to put a check by the quotation to tell yourself that you have reviewed it for accuracy once you have put it down.

Here is a sample note showing direct quotation: If this note were on your computer, you could retrieve it by using "Klan" or "KKK" in your heading and using the search function of your word processing program to bring it up when you needed it. You could then easily append it to your essay:

Wilson mocks fears by blacks of the KKK

"It threw the negroes into a very ecstasy of panic to see these sheeted 'ku klux' move near them in the shrouded night; and their comic fear stimulated the lads who excited it to many an extravagant prank and mummery. No one knew or could discover who the masked players were; no one could say whether they meant serious or only innocent mischief; and the zest of the business lay in keeping the secret close." *History:* 5, 59–60

➜ Wilson seems to enjoy this fear, finds it comic. Regards early Klansmen as comic.

Avoid copying too much as direct quotation in your notes. Writing down the quotation takes time, and you can easily make errors in transcribing it. You save time while you exercise your mind by summary or paraphrase rather than by direct quotation. (Or, if you have the book on interlibrary loan, you may wish to photocopy some pages relevant to your work if you must send the book back before you write the paper.) Paraphrasing is especially valuable if your course is in a foreign language or in a language with a difficult syntax such as early modern English.

As you write, you will probably have Wilson's volumes easily available. When you look at your notes, you can return to the original source and quote it exactly, word for word. Or, to save space, you may say something like this: "Wilson mocked the fear blacks had of the Klan," and you would put in a note the place where the mockery might be found. Here is an example of a summary note:

➜ Wilson mocks black fears of KKK. Seems to enjoy the terror of blacks before the KKK and to regard early Klansmen as pranksters. *History,* 5, 59–60

The third kind of note is your own comment when you read. Comment often as you make notes. Commenting requires you to reflect on what you read, making you an active rather than a passive reader. *Be sure to distinguish between the notes that are your own thoughts and notes that are direct quotations or summaries of your sources.* I put an arrow before one of my own thoughts in my notebook or when I am taking notes on a computer. The arrow lets me know that these thoughts are mine. Many notebook keepers write direct quotations on the right-hand page and keep their own comments on the left-hand page. IF YOU DO NOT TAKE CARE IN DISTINGUISHING YOUR THOUGHTS FROM THE THOUGHTS OF YOUR SOURCE, YOU MAY BE AC-CUSED OF PLAGIARISM. THAT IS AN ACCUSATION FROM WHICH FEW WRITERS CAN RECOVER.

Here is an example of how you might enter a note about your own thoughts.

> → Wilson's view of the Klan goes hand in hand with his general view that blacks have no right to be free of fear or to take part as citizens in the United States. His mention of the "comic" fear of blacks suggests an unconscious appropriation of the common stereotypes, that blacks were either funny or dangerous and in any case that their fears were not to be taken seriously. He barely suggests in the *History* that Klansmen often beat blacks, burned their houses, and sometimes killed them. For Wilson, blacks are always mistreated by *Northerners.* Northerners always mistreat blacks by asking them to assert themselves. Wilson sees blacks as being most happy when they are submissive. He seems to have no sense of the dignity that blacks might lose by being so regarded. *History,* 5, 59–60.

The purpose of such a note is to keep your mind active as you read. A note like this can help shape a major idea for the paper that you will write.

STEP 5: BRAINSTORM AND MAKE AN OUTLINE

Brainstorming is the term we use for making the mind work at a task through a playful, intense forcing out of our thoughts. We may jot down ideas one after another as fast as we can think of them, knowing that we may reject most of them. We may brainstorm in groups by talking hard at each other, trying out ideas, tossing them out to friends and colleagues to see how they fare in open discussion. Brainstorming is an excellent way to arrive at a topic for a history paper.

By the time you have spent two or three afternoons refining your subject, gathering bibliography, and doing spot reading, you will begin to feel more confident about your knowledge. You will have left the somewhat flat and limited accounts of the encyclopedias and other reference books, and you will have started looking at primary sources and specialized books and articles. Your reading should have suggested several interesting topics. You should have asked questions along the way, writing them down in your notebook. You will have noticed patterns or repeated ideas in your research.

Sometimes a pattern occurs in a consistent response to certain subjects. Woodrow Wilson defended the South in writing and in speeches. Why did he do that, and what effect did this attitude have on American history? You may have started with the resolve to write a paper about Woodrow Wilson. If you were lucky, you thought of a limited topic right away, one you might do in 10 or 15 pages. Perhaps, however, you have not been able to limit your topic enough even now. Make a list of interesting topics or problems relating to Wilson. Keep working at it until you arrive at something manageable. The following notes illustrate this attempt to produce both something interesting and something you can do in the time and space available.

"The Civil War in Woodrow Wilson's *History of the American People*." Too vague. Too many topics possible.

"Wilson's Defense of the Ku Klux Klan in his *History of the American People*." Not bad. Wilson's defense of the KKK is surprising, given the popular view that he was liberal for his time. But here the topic seems almost too narrow. Wilson defends the Klan over several pages in his book. He makes some vague comments that indicate disapproval of Klan violence. But they are only vague. No real indignation about that violence. Most of Wilson's *History* is vague. General statements throughout. He tells more of what he felt and believed about the facts rather than what the facts were. Not an impressive piece of work.

The temptation might be to go from Wilson to some general background information about the Klan itself. Then you have to ask questions like these: Do I have the primary sources to study the Klan? Is the topic too big for a paper in my course? Wilson's sympathetic words for the Klan provoke other ideas. What was Wilson's attitude towards blacks in the South and in American society at large? Consult the index in several volumes of the Wilson papers. Slowly read Wilson's comments about blacks in various contexts. Here is much information, and you begin to see patterns. Wilson has no sympathy for the efforts of blacks to vote after the Civil War. He never writes as if blacks and whites are equals. He favors segregation in the federal civil service, especially the Post Office. He insults black leaders who come to visit him at the White House. The major pattern seems clear: Wherever Wilson speaks of race, he assumes the inferiority of blacks and aims at segregation.

Slowly an idea emerges. You adopt a provisional title: "Woodrow Wilson's Attitudes towards Black Americans." You can change a provisional title later. You can change anything in a paper at this stage, and your changes may be sweeping. While you use it, the provisional title gives direction to your work. That sense of direction will help you work faster and more efficiently because it helps organize your thoughts, making you evaluate information you have collected so you can make proper use of it.

If you have done your research well, you cannot use all the information you have collected in your notes. Good writing is done out of an abundance of knowledge. The provisional title will act as a filter in your mind, holding and organizing things you should keep for your essay and letting information go that will not contribute to your argument. And who knows? You may be able to use your surplus in papers you will write later in college or life!

The Outline

Once you arrive at a topic, focus your reading. If you plan to write about Woodrow Wilson's relation to blacks in America, limit yourself to reading only the parts of the Wilson papers and of books about Wilson relating to that subject. You may become so interested in Wilson that you continue to seek other information about him later on. Good! But while you write your paper, limit your reading to texts that help you to your goal.

You may write an outline to help organize your ideas and your evidence. Some writers sit down and start hammering on the keyboard without any clear idea where they are going. If that process works for you, use it. But most people find it more efficient to shape their ideas before they begin to write a draft. You can at least jot down a list of points you want to cover—a list that can be much more flexible than a detailed outline. You can rearrange items on your list as your intuitions suggest better forms of organization. Never be afraid to change a list or outline once you have begun. No matter how clearly you think you see your project in outline before you write a draft, writing may change your ideas. Be ready to follow your mind in its adventures with the evidence. Here is an example of a rough outline for a paper on Woodrow Wilson's attitudes towards black Americans:

> The argument: Woodrow Wilson's attitudes towards blacks, a mixture of paternalism and fear, contributed to racial segregation introduced in the federal civil service early in his presidential administration.
>
> 1. William Monroe Trotter's interview with Wilson in November 1914 on the subject of segregation.
> 2. The larger meaning of the interview.
> 3. Wilson's reasons given to Trotter for accepting racial segregation.
> 4. The deeper explanation—Wilson's lifelong attitudes towards black Americans, attitudes expressed in things he said and wrote long before he became President of the United States.
> 5. Origins: Wilson's romantic view of the South and his admiration for the old Confederacy.
> 6. The attitudes expressed in his *History of the American People.*
> 7. The hostility to blacks by white Southerners Wilson appointed to his cabinet.
> 8. Acceptance of racial segregation by the American people.
> 9. Wilson's segregationist policies and their disastrous effect on race relations in America.

A list outline such as this one avoids a proliferation of Roman numerals and subheadings. You may add subheadings if you want, but you may not need them. Having made a list outline, this writer can write a first draft. He has decided to shape an analytical narrative. That is, he will tell a story and explain its significance for American history. He will tell what happened and who is responsible and why the story is important. Along the way he will tell when and where these happenings took place. And so he can begin.

STEP 6: WRITE SEVERAL DRAFTS

Leave yourself time enough to do several drafts of your paper. If you start writing your paper the day before it is due, stay up all night to do that first draft, and hand it in without having time to revise it, you do an injustice to yourself and your instructor. You may get by, but you may not be proud of your work, and the instructor will probably be bored with it. A hard-pressed instructor, sitting up for hours and hours reading and marking papers from everyone in the class, deserves your best effort.

Note that I am not saying you should not stay up all night long working on your paper before you hand it in. Many writers discover that they get an adrenaline flow from working steadily at a final draft for hours and hours before they give it up, and they may stay up all night because they are excited about their work and cannot leave it. I know what it is to hear the birds begin to sing outside my window at first light before dawn when I have bent over my yellow pad or my keyboard all night long. I like it. That kind of night comes when I have worked hard for a long time, perhaps for years, and feel in command of what I'm doing and want to drive on to the end.

No writer can produce consistently good work by waiting until the last minute to begin. Discipline yourself. When you start writing, stick to it for at least a couple of hours. You may not go very fast. You may consult your notes continually. You may become discouraged. But stay seated, and keep going. The most important task for you in writing your first draft is to make it exist. Get a beginning, a middle, and an end down on paper or on your computer. Write more than you need to write at first. If your assignment is to write a 15-page paper, make your first draft 20 pages. Pack in information. Use quotations. Ruminate about what you are describing. Ask yourself the journalistic questions about your paper, and try to answer them.

When you get your first draft into being, several things happen. You feel an immense relief. An unwritten assignment is more formidable than one you have written—even in a rough draft. You have some idea now what you can say in the space you have available. You have some idea of the major questions you want to address. You know some areas of weakness where you have to do further research. You can see which of your conclusions seem fairly certain and which seem shaky. You can see if you have an idea that binds all your data together into a thesis, a controlling motive that resolves or defines some puzzle that you find in your sources. You can now revise.

Revision proceeds in various ways. If you write with a computer and a word processing program, you can bring your paper up on the screen and start working back through it, inserting, deleting, and changing around the order of the paper. (It's a good idea to make a back-up copy of that first draft so that if you cut something you decide you want to restore later on, you can do so without pain.) Many writers like to print out a draft and go over it with a pen or pencil, making changes that they then type into the draft on the computer. Some research has shown that the longer people work with computers, the more they tend to do their revising directly from the screen without printing out. (I have come back to printing out a manuscript, going over it carefully with a fine-point pen, and inserting corrections and revisions in the computer.) You have to use the method that suits you best. The main task is to read your work over many times. As you read, ask yourself questions. Here is my own list. You may add some of your own.

A Writer's Checklist

✔ What is my major motive for writing this essay? What do I want to prove?

✔ What would draw a modern reader to this essay? What audience do I want?

✔ Do I quote, summarize, and paraphrase sources that demonstrate support for my point of view? Do I have evidence for my argument?

✔ Do I provide enough context to allow readers less informed than I am to follow my essay easily? Can the essay stand alone for the generally educated reader?

✔ Have I classified my evidence? That is, have I placed similar kinds of evidence in the same section of my paper so that readers will not have the feeling of being jerked randomly from one subject to another?

✔ Where do I infer conclusions from the evidence? That is, where do I interpret the evidence instead of being content merely to report it?

✔ Do I take contrary evidence into account? Have I been fair in my presentation of the evidence? Have I written in such a way that someone who knows the evidence as well as I do can compliment me for having done a careful job of putting everything together?

✔ Are my transitions effective? Are the sections of my paper fitted together clearly enough to allow readers to move easily from one to the next without losing track of my argument? Or is there a digression, a jump from one idea to another without adequate preparation?

✔ Is my opening interesting enough to draw readers into it even if they are not specialists in the subject?

✔ Does my conclusion mirror my opening in some way? A good essay comes back to the beginning when it concludes. Some words or ideas that drew attention in the first paragraph are repeated in the last. The beginning points towards the end, and by repeating some of the ideas in the beginning, the writer announces the conclusion. Usually one can read the first and last paragraphs of an essay and have a fairly good idea of what the essay is about and the point of view of the writer.

✔ What is my tone in this paper? Do I sound emotional or preachy? Do I sound belligerent? Do I sound more certain than I really am?

✔ Are there muddled sentences in this draft? Are my sentences clear enough to be understood at first reading? Can I make some of them more simple by eliminating cumbersome phrases or clauses?

✔ Can I eliminate words, phrases, sentences, or whole paragraphs? Is every word necessary if I am to express the meaning I want? Can I make my writing more direct? Can I cut out irrelevant information?

✔ Can I make some sentences more vivid by using the active rather than the passive voice?

✔ Do I repeat some words or phrases too often? Can I find other words and phrases to give variety to my prose? Are there echoes in my prose that I can change? That is, do I say things like, "The defendant defended himself," or "The writer wrote," or "Her description described," or "They considered all the considerations in the statement"?

✔ Have I used clichés, those tired expressions used so often that they have lost all power to be vivid? Have I talked about "the cold, hard facts" or a "bolt from the blue" or "dead as a doornail" or the "bottom line" or the "stark reality?"

As I have already said, you can cultivate a good sense of revision by reading your own work again and again. Reading aloud helps. You can sometimes pick out rough places in your prose because they make you stumble in reading them. Reading aloud with inflection and expression will help you catch places where you may be misleading or confusing.

Professional writers often have others read their work and make suggestions about it. Get help from friends—as I have for every edition of this book. Do not ask them, "What do you think of my paper?" They will tell you it's good. Ask them instead, "What do you think I am saying in this paper?" You will sometimes be surprised by what comes out—and you will get some ideas for revision.

For most of us, the drafting process goes on until the last minute. Drafting helps us see all parts of our work more clearly. It helps us see our thinking, our research, our factual knowledge, our expression, and the shape of our ideas. Very often as we write drafts we realize that our thought is flabby or that we suddenly think of contrary arguments we have not thought of before. We revise to take these contrary arguments into account. Reading our work over and over again teaches us to track our own ideas so that we make them flow from one to another without leaving gaps that may hinder readers from making the connections we want them to make.

5

A Sample Research Paper in History

On the following pages is a sample research paper written for a course in American history using the process outlined in Chapter 4. Study the paper. Then study the questions about the paper at the end. Ask these same questions about any paper you write for a history course.

Pay close attention to the format of the paper. Note the title page, the footnotes, and the bibliography. The title page includes the title of the paper, the name of the author, the date the paper is turned in, the name of the course, the time of the class, and the name of the professor. The margins should be set at one inch on all four sides of the page. ALWAYS number pages, but remember that the title page is not numbered, although it is considered page one in the text of your paper.

Woodrow Wilson's Attitudes Toward Black Americans

By Dick Curry

November 13, 1998

American History 221

Professor Marilyn Carmichael Rutledge

MWF 10:00--11:00

The online biography of Woodrow Wilson available on the Internet from the White House describes his character and lists his achievements as the twenty-eighth president of the United States. He remembered the horrors of the Civil War from his childhood in Atlanta when the city was burned. He favored lower tariffs and supported a federal law prohibiting child labor and another limiting the working day for railroaders to eight hours. After trying to keep the United States out of World War I, he reluctantly led the country into the conflict against Germany. In his statement of war aims, he proposed a League of Nations that would settle future international conflicts by negotiation rather than by force. The U.S. Senate rejected the peace treaty, and Wilson suffered a stroke that effectively ended his public career. In this brief and bland summary, part of an online collection of thumbnail biographies of all the American presidents, we find Wilson the martyr to liberal views, a view shared by multitudes of historians.[1]

In this quasi-official pronouncement on an American president we might expect Wilson's dark side to be ignored. His most recent biographer, August Heckscher, follows the traditional, well-beaten path. In Heckscher's view, Wilson was a saint martyred by selfish political enemies who prevented him from leading the United States to support a world order based on peace and justice.[2] Another recent scholar praises Wilson for domestic leadership and achievements unequaled by any other presidents in American history except Franklin D.

---

[1]"Woodrow Wilson: Twenty-Eighth President 1913-1921," (Washington, D.C.: The White House, 1996. Available from http://www.whitehouse.gov/WH/glimpse/presidents/html/ww28.html; accessed 21 November 1997.

[2]August Heckscher, *Woodrow Wilson* (New York: Charles Scribner's Sons, 1991).

Roosevelt and Lyndon B. Johnson.[3] But to set the record straight, we should acknowledge that while Wilson was seeking to make the "world safe for democracy" abroad, he stood steadfastly against real democracy in America, for Woodrow Wilson stood firmly against any idea of civil rights for black Americans. Throughout his life his animus against blacks was blatant. He introduced racial segregation into the Federal Civil Service and thus buttressed legal discrimination against blacks throughout the United States.

In his laudatory biography, Heckscher devotes only three brief and vague paragraphs to Wilson's attitudes towards race.[4] He does not mention by name Wilson's most persistent black critic, William Monroe Trotter of Boston. Nor does Heckscher describe in detail the momentous confrontation between Trotter and Wilson on November 12, 1914, in the White House.

Trotter was a leader in the struggle of black Americans to end racial discrimination in the United States. He read the President an "Address" vigorously protesting the policy of racial segregation recently introduced into the Federal Civil Service, especially the U.S. Post Office. Afterwards the two men entered into heated disagreement. At the end Wilson all but threw Trotter out of the Oval Office.

The incident marked one of the great setbacks in the struggle for racial equality in America, and it revealed Wilson's own attitudes towards black Americans. Perhaps more important, it revealed an American attitude not to be substantially changed until the Civil Rights movement of the 1950s and 1960s, culminating in the Civil Rights Act of 1964.

---

[3]Robert Dallek, "Woodrow Wilson, Politician," The Wilson Quarterly 15, no. 4 (1991): 106-109.

[4]Heckscher, 292-293.

Trotter was spokesman for the National Independent Equal Rights League, a rival to the then fledgling National Association for the Advancement of Colored People. He was an M.A. graduate of Harvard, class of 1895, and the first African American member of the honor society of Phi Beta Kappa. In 1901 he became editor of the *Guardian* in Boston and wrote vigorously against racism in America. With equal vigor he attacked the moderation of both Booker T. Washington and the fledgling National Association for the Advancement of Colored People. By the turn of the century, the states of the Old Confederacy had restricted black voting, imposing poll taxes, literacy requirements, and ownership of property as qualifications for the ballot. Booker T. Washington, founder of Tuskegee Institute, believed that the franchise was not as important to blacks as intellectual and economic improvement. He looked forward to some distant future when blacks might regain the franchise after they had made progress in other areas. Trotter believed that political action by blacks was necessary before any other progress was possible. And political action required blacks to have the vote.[5]

It was an irreconcilable difference. Trotter attacked Washington furiously in the pages of the Guardian. In 1903 when Washington spoke in Boston, Trotter and his sister interrupted the speech and were arrested.[6] Trotter was eventually tried and briefly jailed for his part in the disruption.[7] In 1912 Trotter supported Wilson in the presidential election, which Wilson won only because the Republican Party was divided. Blacks had been Republican since the Civil War when a

---

[5]Stephen R. Fox, *The Guardian of Boston: William Monroe Trotter* (New York: Athenaeum, 1970), 36.

[6]Ibid., 50-52.

[7]Ibid., 57.

4

Republican president, Abraham Lincoln, issued the Emancipation Proclamation. They did not take kindly to Wilson who was both a Democrat and a Southerner. As Arthur S. Link, Wilson's foremost biographer, points out, blacks had reason to be doubtful about Wilson. Josephus Daniels, one of Wilson's early supporters and friends, editor of the *Raleigh News and Observer,* wrote in an editorial of October 1, 1912, that the South voted solidly Democratic out of

> the realization that the subjection of the negro [sic], politically, and the separation of the negro, socially, are paramount to all other considerations in the South short of the preservation of the Republic itself. And we shall recognize no emancipation, nor shall we proclaim any deliverer, that falls short of these essentials to the peace and welfare of our part of the country.[8]

Daniels wrote this editorial in the midst of the 1912 presidential campaign.

Wilson appealed to blacks to support him, and many did--including William Monroe Trotter. Wilson stood for the "little man" and regularly summoned up a moral sense in the American people. One of his most firm beliefs was that statesmen should supply moral leadership to the nation. He opposed the great corporations and argued that the United States existed not for profit, but because God had given the country a special destiny.[9] These were sentiments bound to appeal to blacks whose religious sense was profound and who were among the most oppressed of American citizens.

---

[8]Quoted in Arthur S. Link, *Wilson: The Road to the White House* (Princeton: Princeton University Press, 1947), 501.

[9]Gregory S. Butler, "Visions of a Nation Transformed: Modernity and Ideology in Wilson's Political Thought," *Journal of Church and State* 39, no. 1 (1997): 37-51.

5

Trotter and Wilson met in July 1912. They apparently got on well. Wilson spoke warmly to various black groups about his willingness to deal with blacks "fairly and justly."[10] The statements were equivocal. What is "fair" or "just" to one person may seem unfair and unjust to another. Nevertheless, blacks had little choice, and many supported Wilson. Link points out that Wilson received more black votes than any previous president in history.[11]

Yet Wilson quickly disappointed black supporters. When he took office, Trotter asked him not to appoint Albert Sidney Burleson, a Texan, to be Postmaster General. Burleson had a reputation for hostility to blacks. Wilson appointed him anyway, and on April 11, 1913, little over a month after Wilson assumed office, Burleson told the Cabinet of his intention to segregate blacks and whites in the post office.[12] Wilson seems to have made no objection.

Trotter had personal reasons to be concerned with racial discrimination in the post office. His father James worked at the post office in Boston. The elder Trotter resigned his job in 1882 because a white man was promoted over him.[13] By 1914 Trotter was plainly furious over what he felt was Wilson's betrayal. In November 1913 he led a delegation to the White House, bringing with him a petition with 20,000 signatures protesting segregation. As he would do in the following year, Trotter read an "Address." In it he told Wilson that "Segregation such as barring from the public lavatories and toilets and requiring the use of separate ones must have a reason. The reason can

---

[10]Link, *The Road to the White House,* 502.

[11]Arthur S. Link, *Wilson: The New Freedom* (Princeton: Princeton University Press, 1956), 243-244.

[12]Fox, 169-170.

[13]Ibid., 19.

only be that the segregated are considered unclean, diseased or indecent as to their persons, or inferior beings of a lower order, or that other employees have a class prejudice which is to be catered to, or indulged."[14]

Trotter pointed out that no other ethnic group was segregated and that any of them would regard such segregation as an insult. "If separate toilets are provided for Latin, Teutonic, Celtic, Slavic, Semitic and Celtic Americans, then and then only would African Americans be assigned to separation without insult and indignity."[15] Federal employees had worked together without segregation in the administrations of President Grover Cleveland, Trotter said. And he recalled that when an effort was made to segregate federal employees on racial grounds, Cleveland stopped it.[16]

In 1913, Wilson's response to Trotter was conciliatory. He claimed ignorance and promised to investigate. He assured Trotter that things would be worked out.[17] John Lorance, a writer for *The Boston Daily Advertiser,* reported on December 9 that in consequence of the meeting with Trotter, Wilson was rolling segregation back. Lorance's article expressed a sense of triumph that Wilson had championed the cause of equality. Other Northern papers reflected the same

---

[14]Woodrow Wilson, *The Papers of Woodrow Wilson,* eds. Arthur S. Link and others (Princeton: Princeton University Press), 28:491. Hereafter *The Wilson Papers* will be abbreviated *WP* with the volume and page numbers for each citation.

[15]Ibid., 28:492. The quotation as given here is correct. Trotter used the word "Celtic" twice--perhaps a sign of his background in Boston where an Irish presence was strong and where separate toilets for those of Irish background would doubtless have been considered an outrage.

[16]Ibid., 28:493.

[17]Ibid., 28:496.

7

sentiments.[18] In fact segregation continued. Josephus Daniels was now Secretary of the Navy. William Gibbs McAdoo of Georgia by way of Tennessee was Secretary of the Treasury. Albert Sidney Burleson was Postmaster General. All these men were close to Wilson; all of them were uncompromising segregationists.[19]

So when Trotter returned with another "Address" and another delegation a year later, he was understandably angry. He felt betrayed, and his "Address" amounted to an indictment. Though it maintained an icy courtesy, the fire of outrage burned beneath the surface. He expressed his disappointment in Wilson's record on race. Wilson had promised to help "Afro-Americans," Trotter said. Instead segregation was advancing steadily, and Wilson was doing nothing about it. Trotter recalled the national petition protesting segregation and presented to the President by black Americans a year before. Such segregation existed in "working positions, eating tables, dressing rooms, rest rooms, lockers, and especially public toilets."[20]

Wilson had promised to investigate. Trotter pointed out that despite this presidential promise, segregation had gone on and that in fact it had increased. He reeled off a long list of government departments and structures where segregation was enforced. Trotter said that American "citizens of color" realized "that if they can be

---

[18]Excerpts from the newspaper articles, including a long quotation from Lorance, appear in the notes of *WP*, 28:498-500.

[19]In his article in The *Boston Daily Advertiser*, Lorance wrote, "The most active segregation has been found under Sec. McAdoo of the Treasury Department, under Postmaster General Burleson of the Post Office Department, and under Sec. Daniels of the Navy Department." See *WP*, 28: 499.

[20]*WP*, 31:300.

segregated and thus humiliated by the national government at the national capital the beginning is made for the spread of that persecution and prosecution which makes property and life itself insecure in the South." He pointed out that blacks who had voted for Wilson were now regretting his election. "Only two years ago you were heralded as perhaps the second Lincoln, and now the Afro-American leaders who supported you are hounded as false leaders and traitors to their race. What a change segregation has wrought!" The indignity of segregation robbed blacks of their rights of citizenship, Trotter said. "Fellow citizenship means congregation. Segregation destroys fellowship and citizenship. Consider that any passerby on the streets of the national capital, whether he be black or white, can enter and use the public lavatories in government buildings, while citizens of color who do the work of the government are excluded." Trotter and his delegation were there to ask Wilson to "issue an executive order against any and all segregation of government employees because of race and color and to ask whether you will do so."[21]

Having presented his "Address," Trotter entered into a spirited dialogue with Wilson. If he expected the President to grant his desire, he was quickly disappointed. The American people rejoiced in the "really extraordinary advances" that blacks had made, Wilson said. "But we are all practical men," the President said. Being "practical" meant that everyone had to recognize that the races could not mix. Segregation was installed to eliminate "the possibility of friction." Wilson was sure friction would result if blacks and whites mixed. People should be "comfortable," he thought. Segregationists within the government "did not want any white man made uncomfortable by anything that any colored man did, or a colored man made

---

[21]Ibid., 31:300.

9

uncomfortable by anything that a white man did in the offices of the government." He was assured, Wilson said, that conditions for blacks and whites were separate but equal. "I haven't had time to look at the conditions myself, but I have again and again said that the thing that would distress me most would be that they should select the colored people of the departments to be given bad light or bad ventilation yet worse than the others, and inferior positions, physically considered." Solving the problems between the races was going to take generations, Wilson said. Blacks and whites were equal in that they both had souls, he said. But there was the matter of economic equality--"whether the Negro can do the same things with equal efficiency. Now, I think they are proving that they can. After they have proved it, a lot of things are going to solve themselves."[22]

Trotter asked a question. What did the President think about the humiliation black federal employees had suffered? Wilson claimed not to know of some of the incidents that Trotter mentioned. He suggested that humiliation was all in the mind. "If you take it as a humiliation, which it is not intended as, and sow the seed of that impression all over the country, why the consequences will be very serious. But if you should take it in the spirit in which I have presented it to you, it wouldn't have serious consequences."[23]

Another member of the black delegation, whom the stenographer was unable to identify, protested that whites and blacks had been working together as clerks for fifty years "without distinction and separation based on their race." It was untenable, this person said, to claim that there was any reason to make the separation now. Trotter broke in. Segregation was inevitably a humiliation, he said.

---

[22]Ibid., 31:300-303.

[23]Ibid., 31:303.

> It creates in the minds of others that there is something the matter
> with us--that we are not their equals, that we are not their brothers,
> that we are so different that we cannot work at a desk beside them,
> that we cannot eat at a table beside them, that we cannot go into
> the dressing room where they go, that we cannot use a locker
> beside them, that we cannot even go into a public toilet with them.

There was no friction in going to a public toilet, he said. Black government workers had been going to public toilets for fifty years. But when the Wilson administration came in, Trotter said, ''a drastic segregation was put into effect at once.'' This segregation was not caused by friction; it was caused by prejudice on the part of the official who put it into operation.[24]

Wilson broke in here, obviously angry. He condemned Trotter's tone. No one had ever spoken to him like that in the White House before, he said. If this organization wished to speak to him again, it had to have another spokesman. ''You have spoiled the whole cause for which you came,'' he told Trotter.[25]

Trotter insisted that he was telling the truth about what blacks in America believed about Wilson and segregation. But Wilson gave not an inch. When Trotter implied that blacks would not vote for Wilson again, Wilson dismissed the threat as ''blackmail'' and concluded, ''You can vote as you please provided I am perfectly sure that I am doing the right thing at the right time.'' With that Wilson broke off the meeting.[26]

So the conversation ended in failure. *The New York Times,* in a story headlined, ''President Resents Negro's Criticism,'' reported the next day that Wilson would continue the segregation begun during his administration. Trotter expressed his disappointment in the meeting

---

[24]Ibid., 31:304-305.

[25]Ibid., 31:306.

[26]Ibid., 31:308.

and announced a mass meeting to be held the following Sunday.[27] A number of newspaper editorials in the North condemned Wilson's policies. Oswald Garrison Villard, editor of the *New York Evening Post* wrote, "The Wilson Administration went out of its way to create the issue it now deplores, and cannot see its way clear to admitting its mistake and reverting to the only defensible position of absolute equality in Government Service."[28]

Wilson held his ground and apparently never reconsidered his position. Had Trotter and others investigated Wilson's past utterances on the subject of race, they might never have entertained the expectations that were now so keenly disappointed.

Wilson was a Southerner, born in Staunton, Virginia, in 1856. His father, Joseph Ruggles Wilson, was a Presbyterian minister. Less than a year after young Woodrow (christened Thomas Woodrow Wilson, he was called Tommy in those days) was born, the Wilsons moved to Augusta, Georgia, and it was there that he passed the Civil War. Link says this about Wilson's sense of being Southern:

> In later life Wilson developed a romantic and extravagant love for the South of legend and song. His letters and addresses are full of expressions of deep feeling for the region. He was one historian, for example, who was not apologetic about the South's history. On one occasion he declared that there was "nothing to apologize for in the history of the South--absolutely nothing to apologize for."[29]

That history, of course, included slavery. And Link says, "He was characteristically a Southerner in his attitude toward the Negro. Like

---

[27]The summaries of these newspaper stories are presented as footnotes to *WP,* 31:308-309.

[28]Editorial of Nov. 17, 1914, quoted in a note in *WP,* 31:328.

[29]Link, *The Road to the White House,* 2.

most Southerners of the upper class, his tolerance of and kindliness to the Negro were motivated by a strong paternalistic feeling."[30]

Paternalism and kindliness meant that although Wilson did not believe in violence towards blacks, he thought they should be kept in an inferior status until some unspecified time when they might have earned some rights to general advancement. Link's "paternalism" scarcely expresses the extent of Wilson's sense that blacks did not know what was good for them and had to be regulated by discreet and wise white men.

Wilson saw blacks in the South as politically incompetent. In an article he tried and failed twice to publish in 1881, Wilson explained the solidity of the old Confederacy behind the Democratic Party. It was all caused by the enfranchisement of blacks. Black voting has been solidly Republican. Southern whites were thus presented with two choices--"to be ruled by an ignorant and an inferior race, or to band themselves in a political union not to be broken till the danger had passed."[31]

Were blacks born inferior, or were they made inferior by their environment? Wilson was unclear on the point. He quoted with favor the sentiments of a Virginian named A. H. H. Stuart who had recently written that Southerners opposed "ignorant suffrage entirely irrespective of race or color. . . . We object to their votes because their *minds* are dark--because they are ignorant, uneducated, and incompetent to form an enlightened opinion on any of the public questions which they may be called on to decide at the polls."[32] There were, Wilson said in conclusion, some blacks who had become "extensive land holders and industrious farmers of their own lands," and these people appeared the

---

[30]Ibid., 3.

[31]*WP*, 2:51-52.

[32]Ibid., 2:51.

start of "an exceedingly valuable, because steady and hardy, peasantry."[33]

The South was striving, he thought, to lift blacks "from degradation."[34] If the Republican party would accept the situation in the South, the fears of Southern whites would be mollified. It is difficult to know if these sentiments represented genuine conviction that blacks could be uplifted until most of them might have the vote. His mention of a "steady and hardy peasantry" may be an almost subconscious statement of how far Wilson expected blacks to advance--to a position of recognizable worth but just as recognizable inferiority. He gave no indication anywhere that he expected blacks to rise to business or the professions. Certain it is that he expected blacks to improve themselves first and only then to be allowed to vote. He expected this process to require a very long time. Since progress was underway (he thought) but nowhere near complete, his energies went to restricting black participation in political life.

These sentiments of the young Wilson did not change. He believed the United States should welcome immigrants "of the right sort," and he favored giving them citizenship and the vote as a means of hastening their assimilation. But he never spoke out in favor of the vote for Southern blacks who did not have it.[35] Nothing shows his attitudes better than his mature work, his *A History of the American People,* published in five volumes in 1901 and 1902. Here he discussed the origins of the Ku Klux Klan in the wake of the Civil War. The Fifteenth

---

[33]Ibid., 2:54.

[34]Ibid., 2:54.

[35]Hans Vought, "Division and Reunion: Woodrow Wilson and the Myth of American Unity," *Journal of American Ethnic History* 13, no. 3 (1994): 27-54.

Amendment, giving the freed slaves the right to vote, ensured that "The dominance of the negroes [sic] in the South was to be made a principle of the very constitution of the Union." It was a "radical Amendment," said Wilson, and it caused "the temporary disintegration of Southern society and the utter, apparently the irretrievable, alienation of the South" from the Republican Party.[36] He wrote not a word to support the view that blacks required the right to vote if they were to make good their freedom.

The Klan grew up, he said, around Pulaski, Tennessee, when young men "finding time hang heavy on their hands . . . formed a secret club for the mere pleasure of association."[37] He described how these young men rode around at night under the moon, wearing white masks and with horses sheeted up like ghosts. The aim of the Klansmen was to frighten blacks. And they succeeded--much to Wilson's evident pleasure:

> It was the delightful discovery of the thrill of awesome fear, the woeful looking for of calamity that swept through the countryside as they moved from place to place upon their silent visitations, coming no man could say whence, going upon no man knew what errand, that put thought of mischief into the minds of the frolicking comrades. It threw the negroes into a very ecstasy of panic to see these sheeted "Ku Klux" move near them in the shrouded night; and their comic fear stimulated the lads who excited it to many an extravagant prank and mummery.[38]

Wilson admitted that things went bad when "malicious fellows of the baser sort who did not feel the compulsions of honor and who had

---

[36]Woodrow Wilson, *A History of the American People* (New York and London: Harper & Brothers, 1901–2), 5:58.

[37]Ibid., 5:59.

[38]Ibid., 5:60.

private grudges to satisfy" imitated the disguises of honorable
Klansmen and did unspecified bad things.[39] It is clear from his account
that he thought that things finally went too far, creating in some places in
the South "a reign of terror."[40]

Yet it is also clear that he sympathized with the original aims of the
Klansmen even if he did not condone their later, more violent methods.
He reported with obvious disapproval an act of Congress of 1871
intended "to crush the Ku Klux Klan and all lawless bands acting after its
fashion." Most startling is Wilson's acquiescence in the breaking of the
law by white Southerners. It was not their law; therefore, he seemed to
say, they were not bound by it. White leaders in the South were shut off
from the ballot, he said. So they had to act in other ways:

> Those who loved mystery and adventure directed the work of the
> Ku Klux. Those whose tastes and principles made such means
> unpalatable brought their influence to bear along every counsel
> of management that promised to thrust the carpet bagger out of
> office and discourage the negro in the use of his vote. Congress
> saw where they meant to regain their mastery, at the polls, and by
> what means, the intimidation and control of the negroes without
> regard to law--the law thrust upon them, not their own; and
> hastened to set up a new barrier of statute against them.[41]

Throughout his discussion of Reconstruction, Wilson took what was
by this time the canonical Southern view: Reconstruction was an
unmitigated evil thrust upon the South by the victorious North, and the
heart of the evil was the franchise extended to the former slaves. He
never asked questions that might have helped him and his readers
understand why Reconstruction came about. The Southern states had

---

[39]Ibid., 5:62.

[40]Ibid., 5:64.

[41]Ibid., 5:72-74.

been in a rebellion against the authority of the central government. In other societies, the leaders of a vanquished rebellion had usually been shot or hanged and sometimes publicly tortured to demonstrate the futility of rebellion. The defeated Southerners were not treated so cruelly, but the victorious Washington government did have some reason to put the former secessionist states on probation. Depriving former rebels of the vote was better than depriving them of their lives. But to Wilson the historian, the Republican party in charge of Reconstruction was dastardly to the core and its measures wicked because they attempted to make full citizens of blacks who had so long been in bondage. Since the Reconstruction measures were imposed on the South by force, Southerners had no moral obligation to obey them.

Though Wilson never quite praised or condoned the violence of Klansmen and others, he did explain it and excuse it. Clearly in his view of things, violence was a lesser evil than black suffrage. He was particularly indignant at Charles Sumner, the Senator from Massachusetts, who had been before the war an abolitionist and after the war an advocate of federal support of black rights in the South. Sumner, said Wilson, insisted that blacks have "social rights" as well as political rights.[42]

What were these "social" rights? They were incorporated in the Act of Congress of February 1875, that "gave the federal courts the authority, by appropriate process and penalty, to enforce the right of negroes to accommodation in public inns, theatres, railway carriages, and schools, and to service upon all juries, upon the same footing as white persons."[43] For Wilson "social" rights clearly included any public association of blacks and whites on grounds of apparent equality. In

---

[42]Ibid., 5:97.

[43]Ibid., 5:98.

short, Wilson the historian advocated the segregation of the races not legally ended until the Civil Rights legislation of the 1960s. The 1875 Act, Wilson wrote, "For eight years . . . was to fail utterly of accomplishing its object and yet to work its work of irritation, to be set aside at last by the Supreme Court (1883) as an invasion of the legal field of the States which no portion of the constitution, new or old, could be made to sustain."[44] The word "irritation" seems significant in view of Wilson's later use of the word "friction" in his discussions with William Monroe Trotter.

Wilson believed that any association of blacks and whites in the workplace, in schools, or on public transportation was bound to create problems. This was the unexamined principle behind all his pronouncements on relations between the races. Therefore, the states, and the federal bureaucracy, could segregate the races. In his interview with Trotter in 1914, Wilson was unwilling to consider that the humiliation felt by blacks under segregation had anything to do with the matter. The humiliation was not intended; Wilson's view was that blacks should accept his own good intentions and make the best of them. Southerners had been entitled to break the law in their wish to enforce segregation; Wilson felt entitled to make rules to the same end.

Most striking in Wilson's *A History of the American People* is how vague it all is. Wilson intended his book for the broad general public. Today such a writer would tell illustrative anecdotes about people. Wilson almost never told an anecdote. His statements remain assertions that we are to believe on account of his authority. He gives us little reason to accept that authority. We learn that things were done, but we never learn the mechanism by which they were done. Only now and then does some specific detail break the monotony of tedious assertion.

---

[44]Ibid., 5:98.

In describing Grover Cleveland, Wilson wrote, "He was of the open and downright sort that all men who love strength must always relish."[45] He did not tell us that Cleveland had sired a son out of wedlock, a fact well known to the public, a story that might have added some content to the vague adjective "downright." In describing the settling of Oklahoma, Wilson came as close as he ever did to specific occurrence: "At noon on the 22d of April, 1889, at the sound of a bugle blown to mark the hour set by the President's proclamation, the waiting multitude surged madly in, and the Territory was peopled in a single day."[46] The concreteness of that lonely bugle is almost startling in Wilson's interminable catalogues of empty generalizations.

This vague generality in his writing of history fitted generalizations-- we can call them stereotypes--he could make about blacks. If his mind had been turned towards the specific, he might have told some stories about responsible, intelligent blacks turned away from the polls by ignorant and violent Southern whites. He might have told stories about victims of the Ku Klux Klan that could have inspired indignation and sympathy not only in readers but in himself. Such stories, had he been interested in them, might have made him at least relax some of the rigor of his views. If we know that a specific man in a specific place has been cruelly denied the vote (no women, black or white, voted in America at that time), and if we know all the details of that denial and of the suffering of the would-be voter, we naturally spring to sympathy with his loss of rights. But Wilson protected his prejudices by throwing around them a wall of authoritative general statement that made them sound like virtues, not only to readers but to himself.

---

[45]Ibid., 5:171.

[46]Ibid., 5: 212.

Individual blacks did not appear in his pages. Indeed individuals scarcely appeared at all except to have their names called if they were men recognized as leaders who needed to have something general said about them.

It should be said that his prejudices were not against blacks alone. Wilson's own ancestry was north European. When he taught at Bryn Mawr and at Princeton, he offered courses in the history of England and France. When he came to discuss immigration in the later nineteenth century, he wrote:

> Throughout the century men of the sturdy stocks of the north of Europe had made up the main strain of foreign blood which was every year added to the vital working force of the country, or else men of the Latin-Gallic stocks of France and northern Italy; but now there came multitudes of men of the lowest class from the south of Italy and men of the meaner sort out of Hungary and Poland, men out of the ranks where there was neither skill nor energy nor any initiative of quick intelligence; and they came in numbers which increased from year to year, as if the countries of the south of Europe were disburdening themselves of the more sordid and hapless elements of their population, the men whose standards of life and of work were such as American workmen had never dreamed of hitherto."[47]

Wilson's ideas about democracy assumed that only certain classes and certain people were worthy of self-government. Arthur S. Link, devoted as he was to Wilson, discussed this aspect of Wilson's career with obvious pain. Wilson himself finally admitted to approving of segregation in government departments, claiming that it was "distinctly to the advantage of the colored people themselves."[48] Support for

---

[47]Ibid., 5:213.

[48]Link, *The New Freedom,* 251.

segregation from the President was bound to have a powerful effect, and to Wilson belongs much of the blame for the failure of the federal government to support the black struggle for equal rights until it was forced to do so by the Supreme Court, the Civil Rights movement led by the Rev. Martin Luther King, Jr., and many others, culminating finally in the Civil Rights Act of 1964.

As Link pointed out, Wilson was not alone in his prejudices. Many newspapers and leaders spoke out against Wilson's segregationist policies. But, said Link, speaking of Wilson's Cabinet, "If there were any opponents of segregation in the Cabinet, they did not then or afterward raise their voices."[49]

Despite some protests against segregation, a majority of whites in America supported discrimination. The year after Wilson's last meeting with William Monroe Trotter, D.W. Griffith brought out his *Birth of a Nation,* glorifying the Ku Klux Klan and portraying blacks as ignorant, malicious, arrogant, and lusting after white women. The film quoted Woodrow Wilson's *A History of the American People* to justify the Klan. It was shown in the White House, though Link holds that Wilson did not thereby endorse the film. Even so, Wilson refused to condemn the film publicly. To do so, he said privately, would be to appear "to be trying to meet the agitation . . . stirred up by that unspeakable fellow Tucker."[50] "Tucker" was Trotter; Wilson got his name wrong. In April 1915, Trotter was charged with assault in Boston when he was refused in his request to buy a ticket for the film, which he may have intended to disrupt.[51] Wilson evidently had this incident in mind, and he could not

---

[49]Ibid., 247.

[50]Ibid., 253.

[51]*Focus on the Birth of a Nation,* ed. Fred Silva (Englewood Cliffs, N.J: Prentice-Hall, 1971), 72-73.

bring himself to do anything that might seem to support Trotter's position.

Others were bolder. In May 1915 former President Charles W. Eliot of Harvard spoke to a mass meeting on the Boston Common about *Birth of a Nation.* He condemned the "dangerously false doctrine" taught by the film "that the Ku Klux Klan was on the whole a righteous and necessary society for the defense of Southern white men against black Legislatures led by Northern white men." Said Eliot, "Undoubtedly, grievous conditions existed in the South, but they did not justify the utter lawlessness and atrocities which marked the trail of the Ku-Klux. There can be no worse teaching, no more mischievous doctrine than this, that lawlessness is justified when necessary."[52]

The philosophy Eliot condemned happened to be the express view of the President of the United States about the Klan. Though Wilson did not formally endorse the film, the quotation of his work in the film itself was an endorsement of the film's fundamental message. Nothing, not even violent lawlessness, seemed as bad to Wilson as blacks in control, and surely they would be in control in many Southern states if they were given equality with whites.

The popularity of the film was in part testimony to Griffith's cinematic genius. But the record of the country at large in Civil Rights shows that the popularity was also testimony to a racial prejudice of the American people that was to rule for decades. Woodrow Wilson's influence on race relations was pernicious. His meeting with William Monroe Trotter in November 1914 was a disaster for Wilson's long-term reputation, but more important, it represented an immediate calamity for blacks facing a president who thought he was doing good. A sadder realization is that Wilson undoubtedly represented the views

---

[52]Ibid., 73.

of most Americans in his day. Trotter received vigorous support from a few Northern papers and liberal groups. None of these counted so much at the time as the conviction of most American whites that Woodrow Wilson's prejudices represented truth. If the thumbnail biography of Wilson available online from the White House told the whole story, it would say that both Woodrow Wilson and the white Americans he represented failed to see the consequences of writing into law a pattern of discrimination that would have disastrous effects for American society.

Bibliography

Butler, Gregory S. "Visions of a Nation Transformed: Modernity and Ideology in Wilson's Political Thought." *Journal of Church and State* 39, no. 1 (1997): 37-51.

Dallek, Robert, "Woodrow Wilson, Politician." *The Wilson Quarterly* 15, no. 4 (1991): 106-109.

Focus on The Birth of a Nation. ed. Fred Silva. Englewood Cliffs, N.J.: Prentice-Hall, 1971.

Fox, Stephen R. *The Guardian of Boston: William Monroe Trotter.* New York: Athenaeum, 1970.

Heckscher, August. *Woodrow Wilson.* New York: Charles Scribner's Sons, 1991.

Link, Arthur S. *Wilson: The New Freedom.* Princeton: Princeton University Press, 1956.

_____. *Wilson: The Road to the White House.* Princeton: Princeton University Press, 1947.

Vought, Hans. "Division and Revision: Woodrow Wilson and the Myth of American Unity." *Journal of American Ethnic History* 13, no. 3 (1994): 27-54.

Wilson, Woodrow. *A History of the American People.* New York and London: Harper & Brothers, 1901-2, vol. 5.

_____. *The Papers of Woodrow Wilson.* Eds. Arthur S. Link and others. Princeton: Princeton University Press, vol. 2, 1967; vol. 28, 1978; vol. 31, 1979.

"Woodrow Wilson: Twenty-Eighth President 1913-1921." Washington, D.C.: The White House, 1996. Available from http://www.whitehouse.gov/WH/glimpse/presidents/html/ww28.html. Accessed 21 November 1997.

THINGS TO NOTICE ABOUT THIS PAPER

This paper presents primary sources, secondary sources, and the interpretations of the author to arrive at a thesis: President Woodrow Wilson made federal government policy according to his belief that black Americans were inferior to whites. The paper is more than a mere sticking together of sources. The writer has thought about the material and has arrived at some interpretations that help explain it. He has inferred much from his texts. Wilson does not say, "I heartily approve of the Ku Klux Klan." But he writes about the Klan in such a way that the writer feel justified in inferring that Wilson thought that the Klan was a better choice than giving black Americans the vote.

The author's own point of view is unmistakable: He laments the decisions Wilson made to enforce racial segregation in America. Yet he does not pour out invective on Wilson's head; he does not preach to us. A historian can make judgments on whether certain actions in the past were good or bad. Historians do that sort of thing all the time. But it is not acceptable in the field of history to rage about events in the past as if our readers must be more persuaded by our emotions than by our evidence and our reasoning. Trust your readers. It is sufficient to point out what Wilson said and did without making vehement denunciations of Wilson himself. Readers can see that Wilson harmed the cause of equality in America, and they can make up their own minds about his character. We have a right to be angry with Wilson after studying the evidence. Yet anger does no good in the writing of history, and it can irritate readers so much that they stop reading. A reader does not read this paper to see how angry the writer is; the reader reads to see what Wilson did and why.

The paper moves steadily to develop its thesis. When new information is presented, we are told immediately how that information relates to the thesis of the paper. We are not left wondering. The paper is documented throughout so we can look up the evidence if we want to know more about it. The emphasis on primary sources helps prevent the paper from being a collage of what others have said about Wilson. The thoughtfulness of the author in dealing with his sources is enough to make us feel that we have learned something important from someone who has taken pains to become an authority in this area of Wilson's life and thought.

Answer the questions below by studying the sample paper. Apply these questions to your own writing:

1. What sentence or sentences near the beginning of the paper announce the writer's thesis, the main idea that controls the paper?

2. How does the writer use quotations? How many block quotations are in the paper? Why does he use block quotations here and there and shorter quotations elsewhere?
3. What is the form of the footnotes? Why does the form sometimes change?
4. Where does the writer use secondary sources? Can you show where he disagrees with some of his secondary sources?
5. Where does the author make inferences? That is, where does he make plausible suggestions about the meaning of various texts when the meaning is not explicit in the text itself?
6. Where are narrative paragraphs in the essay?
7. Where are expository paragraphs in the essay?
8. Where are arguments in the essay?
9. Where does the writer make his own judgments clear?
10. In what ways does the conclusion of the paper mirror some ideas in the opening?
11. How would you describe the opening of the paper?
12. Are any of the writer's sentences especially well written?

6

Documenting Your Sources

When you write about history—or any other topic that requires research—you must use documentation that will allow your readers to check your sources. You know by now that historians depend on primary and secondary sources as they produce their stories of the past, that indeed to write history is always to write about sources. Other historians want to be able to check the evidence to see if the writer has cited it accurately and interpreted it soundly. Historians also use the documentation in books and articles they read to help them in their own research.

When you quote from a source or use information gathered from a source, tell your readers where to find the quotation or the information. When you quote the exact words of a source, enclose those words in quotation marks or use a block quotation to let readers know where you found them. If you summarize or paraphrase a source, let readers know what you are doing. Otherwise you may be guilty of plagiarism, and remember always that plagiarism is the writer's unpardonable sin. In the typical history paper, you will have many more footnotes to ideas and paraphrased information than you will to direct quotations.

Here are some simple rules to avoid plagiarism and to help you know when to acknowledge that you have taken information from a source.

1. Use a footnote, an endnote, or a mention in your text whenever you quote directly from a source.

A good rule of thumb is to provide the source of any quotation of three or more successive words. Use quotation marks to show that you are quoting. Here is a text from a secondary source, Frederick A. Pottle's *James Boswell: The Earlier Years 1740–1769*. Pottle speaks of Samuel Johnson, author of the first great English dictionary:

> Johnson was at this time in his fifty-fourth year, a huge, slovenly, near-sighted scholar, his face scarred by scrofula, his body distorted by com-

pulsive tics, his speech interspersed with absent-minded clucks and mutterings.[1]

You might cite part of this text with a direct quotation followed by a footnote:

> When Boswell met him, Johnson was fifty-four years old, "a huge, slovenly, near-sighted scholar, his face scarred by scrofula, his body distorted by compulsive tics, his speech interspersed with absent-minded clucks and mutterings."[1]

Or you can attribute your source within your own text like this:

> Frederick A. Pottle says that when Boswell met him, Johnson was fifty-four years old, "a huge, slovenly, near-sighted scholar, his face scarred by scrofula, his body distorted by compulsive tics, his speech interspersed with absent-minded clucks and mutterings."[1]

Your teacher may ask you to write a short paper without footnotes or endnotes—a brief report, a position paper, a summary of your knowledge on a topic. Even without footnotes and endnotes, you can show in your text that you are quoting someone else's work. You can say, "According to Natalie Zemon Davis . . ." or you can say, "Caroline Walker Bynum thinks that . . . ."

2. Acknowledge any paraphrase or summary you make of someone else's thoughts.

Here is a paragraph from *The Hour of Our Death,* by Phillippe Ariès, a history of attitudes towards death in the Western world. Here Ariès writes about the denial of death in the nineteenth century when people took a sentimental attitude towards death:

> Since death is not the end of the loved one, however bitter the grief of the survivor, death is neither ugly nor fearful. On the contrary, death is beautiful, as the dead body is beautiful. Presence at the deathbed in the nineteenth century is more than a customary participation in a social ritual; it is an opportunity to witness a spectacle that is both comforting and

[1]New York: McGraw-Hill, 1985, 113.

exalting. A visit to the house in which someone has died is a little like a visit to a museum. How beautiful he is! In the bedrooms of the most ordinary middle-class Western homes, death has come to coincide with beauty. This is the final stage in an evolution that began very quietly with the beautiful recumbent figures of the Renaissance and continued in the aestheticism of the baroque. But this apotheosis should not blind us to the contradiction it contains, for this death is no longer death; it is an illusion of Art. Death has started to hide. In spite of the apparent publicity that surrounds it in mourning, at the cemetery, in life as well as in art and literature, death is concealing itself under the mask of beauty.[2]

Here is a way to summarize this passage. The summary would require a footnote or an endnote:

> Phillippe Ariès tells us that in the sentimental nineteenth century, the terror of death was hidden under a cult of the beautiful. People gathered at the deathbed as if to share an exalting occasion, and after death the corpse was admired for its beauty. Such rituals were ways of hiding death by covering it with illusions. The thought seemed to be that if people could put a beautiful mask on death, it would cease to seem so horrible.

The ideas here clearly come from the book by Ariès, even though they do not directly quote him. The author *must* footnote Ariès saying, in effect, "This is where I got these ideas." Let me repeat. This kind of note will usually be much more common in your papers than the footnote to a direct quotation. That is, you will paraphrase or summarize much more frequently than you quote directly.

Important ideas remain in some sense the property of the people who shape them and convey them to the world. You would not dream of writing about Sir Isaac Newton's laws of motion or Albert Einstein's theory of relativity as if you had discovered these ideas on your own. In much the same way, ideas about past events belong to the thinkers who conceived them, and you must acknowledge them when you use them in your own work. We have noted comments by Phillippe Ariès on nineteenth-century sentimental attitudes about death. His ideas may be help-

---

[2]Phillippe Ariès. *The Hour of Our Death,* trans. Helen Weaver (New York: Vintage Books, 1982), 473.

ful in understanding the enormous popularity of Tennyson's poem "Crossing the Bar," written in the nineteenth century, if you wrote a paper on the subject. You should certainly give Ariès credit, even if you do not quote him word for word in your own essay.

You do not have to give sources for common knowledge. Nor do you need a note for common expressions of allusions. You don't have to tell people that the sentence, "Pride goeth before destruction," comes from the Bible or that "To be or not to be" comes from Shakespeare's *Hamlet.* If you are not sure whether some piece of information or an idea is common knowledge, ask your teacher or a reference librarian for an opinion.

3. Use forms of notes that allow readers to find your sources easily.

You can check Dick Curry's essay on Woodrow Wilson to see variations on footnote forms. All the notes in that paper are footnotes, but they could just as well have been placed at the end of the paper as endnotes.

Forms of notes vary. Often schools or individual teachers have a style of footnote or endnote that they require, and you should observe that style carefully. The same is true with many scholarly journals that require a particular style. It has been more common in my own experience, both as a student and as a faculty member, that most instructors simply ask students to be consistent. A number of style manuals providing forms for footnotes and endnotes are in print, and English handbooks used in freshman composition courses always have sections on writing research papers. These sections include footnote style.

The most comprehensive and authoritative manual for style and mechanics is *The Chicago Manual of Style,* issued by the University of Chicago Press and now in its fourteenth edition, published in 1993—and doubtless to have received another edition by the time this book appears. Generations of students have used Kate L. Turabian, *A Manual for Writers of Term Papers, Theses, and Dissertations,* published by the University of Chicago Press and now in its sixth edition, that of 1996. Turabian's work, a conveniently sized paperback, represents a condensation of the hefty *Chicago Manual of Style.* Because Turabian's book is so widely used in colleges and universities, I have adopted her style with its parentheses and colons in this book of mine.

Yet I recall that when I entered Yale University to do graduate work in church history in 1958, we were given a couple of pages of simplified sample footnotes where the only punctuation marks were commas and periods—except, of course, for whatever punctuation marks appeared in the titles of works we cited. I have followed that simplified style in my dissertation on Thomas More finished in 1962 and in my writing for all these years since without ever receiving a complaint from editors or readers. That style would note Turabian's work like this:

> [1]Kate L. Turabian, *A Manual for Writers of Term Papers, Theses, and Dissertations,* 6th edition, Chicago, University of Chicago Press, 1993, p. 15.

Whatever the style, footnotes and endnotes must be consistent, and they must lead readers to the precise location of material that is quoted or summarized in a paper. Notes to books must include the name of the writer, the complete title, the name of the editor and/or translator if there is one, the place where the book was published, the name of the publisher, the date, and the page number where the quoted or mentioned material is found. (Increasingly in footnotes in scholarly books the name of the publisher is omitted, the thought being that it is unlikely that two books with the same title would be published at the same time in the same city and need, therefore, to be distinguished from one another.) The complete title should be in italics if you use a word processor on a computer, or if you use a typewriter, the title should be underlined. If a book appears in a series, some style manuals suggest that the name of the series also be mentioned. If the work is in several volumes, as is Woodrow Wilson's *A History of the American People,* the volume number used as a source should be given.

SAMPLE FOOTNOTES

Books

Here are some sample footnote references to books. (Endnotes are in the same style as footnotes; the only difference is that endnotes go at the end of the paper, before the bibliography.) The notes here are in the Turabian style.

A book with a single author:

> [1]Caroline Walker Bynum, *The Resurrection of the Body in Western Christianity, 200-1336* (New York: Columbia University Press, 1995), 13.

A book with more than one author:

[2]Stanley L. Engerman and Robert William Fogel, *Time on the Cross: The Economics of American Negro Slavery* (New York: Norton, 1989), 206.

A book in a series:

[3]Larry William Moses and Stephen A. Halkovic, Jr., *Introduction to Mongolian History and Culture,* Indiana University Uralic and Altaic Series, vol. 149 (Bloomington: Research Institute for Inner Asian Studies, Indiana University, 1985), 199.

A book that has been edited and/or translated:

[4]Martin Luther, *Lectures on Romans,* ed. and trans. Wilhelm Pauck (Philadelphia: The Westminster Press, 1961), 100.

An article in a book that is a collection of essays:

[5]A. W. Reed, "William Rastell and More's English Works," *Essential Articles for the Study of Thomas More,* eds. R.S. Sylvester and G.P. Marc'hadour (Hamden, Connecticut: Archon Books, 1977), 437.

Periodicals

Periodicals are, as the name indicates, published at regular intervals, and under that heading we include scholarly journals, popular magazines, and newspapers. In footnoting periodicals you must include the author, the title of the article, the date of publication, and the page numbers of the information you cite. Turabian recommends including volume number and even issue number as in the following:

[6]Denise S. Spooner, "A New Perspective on the Dream: Midwestern Images of Southern California in the Post-World War II Decades," *California History* 76, no. 1, Spring 1997: 48.

The journal *California History* paginates every issue separately. Many journals, such as *The American Historical Review,* paginate consecutively

through the year so that the first issue begins with page 1 and the last issue may end with page 1250, or whatever. In that case, Turabian recommends omitting the issue number.

Many publishers in these days of skyrocketing costs omit both volume number and issue number, leaving only the date which I have always found sufficient to locate the reference. Issues of popular magazines
such as *Time, Newsweek,* and *Smithsonian* are always identified by the
date alone.

Popular magazine, paginated by issue:

[7]Janet Wallach, "Daughter of the Desert," *Smithsonian,* April 1998,

125.

Newspapers are often published in sections. In the following note,
the "A1" refers to section A, page one.

Newspaper article:

[8]David E. Sanger, "Clinton Warns Japan: Fire Up Economy to Stem

a Decline," *New York Times,* April 4, 1998, A1.

Book Reviews

Notes that refer to book reviews should begin with the name of the reviewer, followed by the title of the book reviewed and the publication
data of the journal where the review appears:

[9]Harvey Hames, review of *Rituals of Childhood: Jewish Acculturation*

in Medieval Europe, by Ivan G. Marcus, *Journal of Jewish Studies* 48

(Autumn 1997): 387.

Notice, too, that a source used many times in a paper may be abbreviated
after the first reference. The paper by Dick Curry included in Chapter 5
cites *The Papers of Woodrow Wilson,* indicated by the letters *WP* for
"Wilson Papers." Note that the letters *WP* are in italics.

Successive Quotations
from the Same Source

When you cite a book or an article after your first note to that source in
your essay, you need put only the author's name and the page number.

Readers will assume that you refer to the same work you have previously footnoted. If you quote or allude to several books by the same author, you must put a short title after the author's name to indicate which of the books is meant. Look at the paper by Dick Curry to see how two books by Arthur S. Link are footnoted. Your instructor may prefer that you put a short title in each note after the author's name. In Dick Curry's essay, the short title *History* after the name "Wilson" is used in every note where Woodrow Wilson's *A History of the American People* is meant. Because Wilson wrote so much, it seemed good to keep reminding readers that this was the work referred to here.

Some writers put notes in parentheses within the text of an essay, usually at the end of a sentence like this (Pelikan, 23). The full bibliographic reference to a source is in a list at the end. You can consult the title of the book and the publication data under the entry "Pelikan, Jaroslav" and easily find the reference and look up page 23. I find this kind of annotation distracting. It was designed for typewriters and the hardship of measuring pages to be sure room was left at the bottom for the notes. Word processing programs regularly have splendid footnoting abilities. The computer does all the measuring, and students should tuck the notes there or in endnotes to avoid making readers stumble over unnecessary parentheses.

Online and CD-ROM Materials

The same general principles apply for noting online materials from the Internet and from electronic mail that apply to noting books and articles. Your reader must be able to find the precise reference that you have noted in your work. Some online materials may be essays and even books posted on the Internet, and you should use the title that is used in the source. You should provide the date on which you accessed the information. This is important to annotation because materials on the Internet are much less stable than books and bound periodicals. They may disappear or be changed. You should give the address on the net that can allow anybody to access it, and if your document is long and paginated, you should place the page at the end just as you do for a book or periodical.

Online material:

[10]Thomas More, "The History of King Richard the Third,"

⟨http://www.r3.org/bookcase/more/moretext.html⟩(Feb. 21, 1998), 35.

CD-ROM material:

[11]"Wilson, Woodrow," *Encyclopedia Britannica CD98,* (CD-ROM).

BIBLIOGRAPHIES

Bibliographies are placed at the end of a book or an essay to allow readers to see quickly what works have been cited in the body of the text. A bibliography shows whether the writer has consulted a wide variety of sources and whether he or she knows the latest literature in a field of inquiry. You have seen the bibliography for the paper on Woodrow Wilson in Chapter 5.

Bibliographies comprise much the same information as footnotes, but bibliographies are alphabetized by the last name of the author, and the punctuation is somewhat different. In Turabian's style, the bibliographic entry does not use parentheses. Here is the bibliogaphic entry of the book by Caroline Walker Bynum listed in a footnote above.

Book by a single author:

Bynum, Caroline Walker. *The Resurrection of the Body in Western Christianity, 200-1336.* New York: Columbia University Press, 1995.

Notice the positions of the periods, the absence of parentheses, and the absence of footnote numbers and page numbers. Bibliographic references to periodicals follow the same principles except that the first and last page numbers of articles are included.

Article in a periodical:

Spooner, Denise S. "A New Perspective on the Dream: Midwestern Images of Southern California in the Post-World War II Decades." *California History* 76, no. 1 (Spring 1997): 45-57.

Many instructors like students to indent the second line of a bibliographical reference to make the author stand out. So you get this form:

Spooner, Denise S. "A New Perspective on the Dream: Midwestern Images of Southern California in the Post-World War II Decades." *California History* 76, no. 1 (Spring 1997): 45-57.

A bibliographical entry with multiple authors:

Moses, Larry William, and Stephen A. Halkovic, Jr., *Introduction to Mongolian History and Culture.* Indiana University Uralic and Altaic Series, vol. 149. Bloomington: Research Institute for Inner Asian Studies,

Indiana University, 1985.

A collection of essays by several authors: (The work is alphabetized according to the first word in the title.)

Commonwealth History of Massachusetts. Five volumes. Ed. Albert

Bushnell Hart, New York: The States History Company, 1927, 1928.

Online source:

More, Thomas. "The History of King Richard the Third."

⟨http://www.r3.org/bookcase/more/moretext.html⟩(Feb. 21, 1998).

CD-ROM source:

Wilson, Woodrow. *Encyclopedia Britannica CD98.* (CD-ROM).

The moment one begins to do research and write about it, the more complex footnoting and bibliographies become. Turabian's manual is larger than this book, and as mentioned above, it is only an abridgment of the much larger *Chicago Manual of Style.* The good news is that common sense and care for precision and consistency can solve a multitude of problems and allow writers to guide their readers faithfully through the sources that the writers have used, no matter what those sources may be.

7

Suggestions about Style

Style in writing varies from writer to writer, and general agreement on style is hard to come by. Some historians are vivid and dramatic. Others are content to be more prosaic. Substance is always to be prized over surface in writing history. A beautiful writing style that conveys falsehood does nobody any good. But historians should remember a moral obligation to share their findings with the general public. Knowledge of history is a necessity of democratic government just because so many politicians appeal to history to justify their course of action. "History proves that we must do this or that," they say. Sometimes the best thing a historian can say is this: "History proves no such thing." As I pointed out earlier, such a historian might have had a profound influence on Lyndon Johnson's determination not to be the first president who lost a war. Someone should have pointed out to him the American defeat in Canada in 1812. But then the historian must communicate the reasons for this judgment so readers can understand them.

The best advice is to write clearly enough so readers can understand your work without having you there to explain it to them. Most writers work hard all their lives to develop a style they find both natural and attractive, one that others can understand and enjoy. No writer can please everybody. Shape your own style by making it as readable as you can, trying at the same time to avoid monotony of expression. A good style combines readability and variety without going so far as a variety that is ostentatious.

A brief chapter cannot tell you everything you need to know about style. But since beginning writers often lack confidence in their own writing, a few principles drawn from research on readability and the common practice of many mature writers may help. The following suggestions are meant as guides to the perplexed.

1. Write in coherent paragraphs.
Paragraphs are groups of sentences bound together by a controlling idea. You have been reading paragraphs throughout this book, taking

them for granted because they are common to nearly all prose. Paragraphs help readability. Indentations break the monotony of long columns of type. They help readers follow the text with greater ease, providing special help when we lift our eyes from the page and must find our place again. They signal a slight change in subject from what has gone before. They announce that the paragraph to follow will develop a thought that can usually be summarized in a simple statement.

The paragraph was not defined until the second half of the nineteenth century. Those who did the defining could not agree on how long a paragraph should be. The disagreement persists today. Long paragraphs can become disorganized. Even a well-organized long paragraph may create eye strain. Short paragraphs may give an appearance of choppiness, of shifting from subject to subject without giving readers time to adjust. A good rule of thumb is to have one or two indentations on every typed manuscript page. It is only a rule of thumb—not a divine command. And it is a good idea to avoid the one-sentence paragraph common in journalism.

A lot of nonsense has been written about paragraphs in textbooks. The textbooks tell us that paragraphs have "topic sentences" and that the topic sentence may appear at the beginning, the middle, or the end. But the topic sentence is a myth. All paragraphs are built on the first sentence. It gives the direction the paragraph should take, and the succeeding sentences in the paragraph should run in a natural flow from it.

Here is a paragraph by William Manchester, who in this part of a book on recent American history describes various political figures who became popular immediately after World War II. Manchester tells of Joseph McCarthy who became a U.S. Senator after World War II and became notorious for declaring that the federal government was infested with Communists. He never exposed a Communist, but he damaged many reputations before he was censured by the Senate in 1954 for irresponsible character assassination. He drank himself to death in 1957.

> Joe McCarthy, late of the Marine Corps, was reelected circuit judge in 1945. He immediately began laying plans to stump his state in the following year under the slogan "Wisconsin Needs a Tail Gunner in the Senate," telling voters of the hell he had gone through in the Pacific. In reality McCarthy's war had been chairborne. As intelligence officer for Scout Bombing Squadron 235, he had sat at a desk interviewing fliers who had returned from missions. His only wartime injury, a broken leg, was incurred when he fell down a ladder during a party on a seaplane tender. Home now, he was telling crowds of harrowing nights in

trenches and dugouts writing letters to the families of boys who had been slain in battle under his leadership, vowing that he would keep faith with the fallen martyrs by cleaning up the political mess at home— the mess that had made "my boys" feel "sick at heart." Sometimes he limped on the leg he broke. Sometimes he forgot and limped on the other leg.[1]

The first sentence of this paragraph, *Joe McCarthy, late of the Marine Corps, was reelected circuit judge in 1945,* sets the topic. The second sentence picks up the main thought of the first sentence by using the pronoun *he* and by telling us something else about McCarthy. The third sentence continues the subject by telling us about *McCarthy's war*—and so through the paragraph. We could summarize this paragraph by saying, "Here is a collection of facts about the political rise of Joseph McCarthy after World War II."

In any good paragraph you can draw lines between connectors, words like the pronoun *he* in the paragraph about McCarthy, a pronoun repeated throughout the paragraph. Sometimes the connector will be a word in one sentence that is repeated in the next. The connectors tie your sentences together—and therefore link your thoughts. They keep your ideas and information in an orderly framework. You can often test paragraph coherence by seeing if every sentence has a connector word that joins its thought in some way to the previous sentence all the way back to the first sentence in the paragraph.

The structure of paragraphs is usually either serial or listing. In the *serial* pattern of paragraph development, the second sentence develops a word or thought in the first sentence, the third sentence develops a word or thought in the second sentence, the fourth sentence will develop a word or thought in the third sentence, and so on until the end. In the *list* pattern, sentences in the paragraph make a more or less interchangeable list of items that support the general statement made in the first sentence.

In the serial paragraph, the order of the sentences is difficult or impossible to rearrange because each sentence depends on the one immediately before it. In the list paragraph, the order can usually be rearranged after the first sentence because the sentences that come afterwards have an equal relation to that first sentence. The paragraph

[1]William Manchester, *The Glory and the Dream* (Boston: Little, Brown, 1973), 394.

from William Manchester about Joe McCarthy is a typical serial paragraph. After the first sentence, each succeeding sentence rises naturally from the one before it. You cannot easily rearrange the sentences and preserve the meaning and the tone.

The following paragraph tells us some reasons why Ngo Dinh Diem, the dictator of South Vietnam in 1963, lost his position and his life. The first sentence makes a statement, and the later sentences support it, but they could be rearranged in a different order:

> Diem, though dedicated, was doomed by his inflexible pride and the unbridled ambitions of his family. Ruling like an ancient emperor, he could not deal effectively with either the mounting Communist threat to his regime or the opposition of South Vietnam's turbulent factions alienated by his autocracy. His generals—some greedy for power, others antagonized by his style—turned against him. His end, after eight years in office, came amid a tangle of intrigue and violence as improbable as the most imaginative of melodramas.[2]

Stanley Karnow, the author of this paragraph, begins with Diem's doom; Diem was assassinated. Having mentioned the doom—foretold in earlier parts of his book—Karnow lists reasons for it. He could just as easily have written the paragraph like this:

> Diem, though dedicated, was doomed by his inflexible pride and the unbridled ambitions of his family. His end, after eight years in office, came amid a tangle of intrigue and violence as improbable as the most imaginative of melodramas. His generals—some greedy for power, others antagonized by his style—turned against him. Ruling like an ancient emperor, he could not deal effectively with either the mounting Communist threat to his regime or the opposition of South Vietnam's turbulent factions alienated by his autocracy.

All paragraphs do not fall so neatly into the two categories as these two. Writing is, thank heaven, not so simple. You may have a mixture of serial sentences and listing sentences in the same paragraph. But keeping in mind the distinction may help you keep your own writing more coherent.

[2]Stanley Karnow, *Vietnam: A History* (New York: Penguin Books, 1984), 277.

In good paragraphs and essays (or chapters of books), patterns of repetition hold all prose together. Pronouns, synonyms, and repeated nouns demonstrate that the writer is picking up thoughts from earlier in the work and reasserting them to say more about them. Our short-term memories require this kind of repetition so that as readers we are continually reminded of what has gone on before. Each sentence both repeats something from previous sentences—a word, a synonym, or an idea— while adding something new to the information we already possess.

Again it is worth saying that the first sentence in the paragraph is normative for the rest of it. It sets both the subject and the tone for what follows, and all the other sentences extend its meaning. Sometimes you can find something approximating the standard topic sentence of the English textbooks, a generalization that sums up everything in the paragraph, but often you cannot. Narrative paragraphs are likely to have nothing like the standard topic sentence. One thing happens after another in a series of sentences. Here is a narrative paragraph from Wallace Stegner's *The Gathering of Zion,* his story of the Mormon trail and the journey of Brigham Young's early group of Mormon immigrants to Utah. The "Revenue Cutter" is the name of a small boat the Mormons found operating on the river when they arrived at the crossing. Stegner calls the Mormons "saints" because that is what they called themselves:

> Travelers late in the season often found the North Platte here clear and shrunken and shallow enough to be waded. But in June it was a hundred yards wide and fifteen feet deep, with a current strong enough to roll a swimming horse. (It did in fact drown Myers' buffalo horse.) The Revenue Cutter could carry the wagons' loads, but the wagons themselves were a problem. While some of the saints brought down poles from the mountain and worked at making rafts, others experimented with swinging wagons across the river on a long rope tied to the opposite bank. Two wagons tied together keeled over on striking the far shore, breaking the reach of one and the bows of the other. Four lashed together proved to be stabler, but too heavy to handle. One alone, with an outrigger of poles to steady it, was caught by the current and the strong southwest wind and rolled over and over. The best system appeared to be ferrying one at a time on a clumsy raft. A backbreaking day of that, up to their armpits in icy water, and they had crossed only twenty-three wagons. It rained and hailed on them, and the wind blew. The river was rising so fast they were afraid of being held up for days; and thinking of themselves, they also thought of the great company crowded with women and children who would soon follow them. Brigham put a crew

to hewing two long dugout canoes from cottonwood logs and planking them over to make a solid ferryboat.[3]

The first sentence introduced the North Platte river, and the other sentences give in chronological order the events that took place as the Mormons set out to cross it. Nothing resembling the standard topic sentence is here to be found. Such a sentence is not necessary because the action builds sentence by sentence in a careful pattern of repetition that is clearly understandable.

Although narrative paragraphs seldom have topic sentences, expository paragraphs may begin with a general statement developed in the paragraph itself. Expository paragraphs explain information. We explain documents or people or events by paying attention to details that make up a text, a personality, or a happening. We look at the relation of those details to one another. We try to understand what caused them and what they contribute to the whole. A general statement at the beginning of an analytical paragraph may express the idea that the paragraph will expand.

An article in a recent issue of *The American Historical Review* dealt with the development of shopping malls, or "shopping towns" as some people called them in the 1960s. Here is an analytical paragraph with a general statement that comes at the beginning. Victor Gruen was a developer in New Jersey at the time:

> While bringing many of the best qualities of urban life to the suburbs, these new "shopping towns," as Gruen called them, also sought to overcome the "anarchy and ugliness" characteristic of many American cities. A centrally owned and managed Garden State Plaza or Bergen Mall, it was argued, offered an alternative model to the inefficiencies, visual chaos, and provinciality of traditional downtown districts. A centralized administration made possible the perfect mix and "scientific" placement of stores, meeting customers' diverse needs and maximizing store owners' profits. Management kept control visually by standardizing all architectural and graphic design and politically by requiring all tenants to participate in the tenants' association. Common complaints of downtown shoppers were directly addressed: parking was plentiful, safety was ensured by hired security guards, delivery tunnels and loading courts kept truck traffic away from shoppers, canopied walks and air-conditioned stores made shopping comfortable year 'round, piped-in background music replaced the cacophony of the street. The preponderance of

[3]Wallace Stegner, *The Gathering of Zion* (New York: McGraw Hill, 1964), 148.

chains and franchises over local stores, required by big investors such as insurance companies, brought shoppers the latest national trends in products and merchandising techniques. B. Earl Puckett, Allied Stores' board chair, boasted that Paramus's model shopping centers were making it "one of the first preplanned major cities in America." What made this new market structure so unique and appealing to businessmen like Puckett was that it encouraged social innovation while maximizing profit.[4]

When you explain an idea or an event in history, you will help readers see where you are going if you present a generalization in the first sentence and develop this thought through the rest of the paragraph.

As I have said, the paragraph is a flexible form, and these suggestions about its structure are not rigid rules. But if you think of them when you write, you will develop greater coherence to your thought, and you can develop a feel for what should be in a paragraph and what not.

2. Illustrate major generalizations by specific references to evidence.

In my experience, students love the grand generalizations that seem to explain everything and to give to the student writer an air of authority. But generalizations are tricky business in writing history. The mysteries of the past are infinite and frustrating. We tire of the equivocations scholars make. "This may be true, but there is some evidence against it." "This may be false, but on the other hand, some evidence supports it." We want certainty, firmness, stern moral principles that cannot be violated, truth. And so it is easy for any of us to get caught up in some grand and definite generalization that seems to explain everything. Beware of that temptation!

Often I have had students, especially in freshman courses, who launch grand generalizations like rockets aimed at the moon. "During Reconstruction Yankee carpetbaggers and Southern turncoats called scalawags trampled the prostrate South into the dirt and so ravaged its economy that it could not recover for a century." "The Roman Empire fell because the Romans began to practice birth control and so reduced their population so much that the German tribes were able to make an easy conquest." "Germans are historically more aggressive and militaris-

---

[4]Lizabeth Cohen, "From Town Center to Shopping Center: The Reconfiguration of Community Marketplaces in Postwar America," *The American Historical Review* (October 1996): 1056.

tic and more hostile to minorities than are the other people of Western Europe."

I have seen all these generalizations in papers in my day, and all of them make me reach for the Pepto-Bismol. None of them stands up under careful scrutiny of the evidence. In fact, the evidence makes these grand generalizations sound empty, even a bit foolish. It's easy to forgive young students for these enthusiasms of certainty, but the fact remains that history is endless careful discussion of the evidence, an edifice built brick by brick—and often remodeled while under construction. It is not a discipline that comes prefabricated so that all the history student has to do is take it out of the box and paste it together in a grand form that everybody agrees on before the box is opened.

One of the most important cautions for the budding historian is to avoid making the kind of sweeping generalization that makes readers lose confidence in your knowledge and your judgment. The best way to avoid the pitfalls of overgeneralization is to follow a simple rule: Provide supporting evidence for the generalization, and at the same time try to find any evidence that might seem to contradict your generalization. Be detailed enough in supporting your generalization, and fair enough in testing it so that your readers gain confidence that you know what you are talking about.

If you say that Woodrow Wilson had racist ideas, quote from his works to demonstrate them. Search through his works for any evidence you can find that he was not a racist. The truth of history resides in the details. The details also give life to the past and make us see the connections between past and present. A related point is this: Make only the kind of generalization that you can readily support by details. Details can be quotations, statistics, summaries of events, and any number of other things. Study the paper on Wilson in Chapter 5 to see how Dick Curry supports his generalizations about Wilson with quotations, summaries, and paraphrases of the sources.

3. To test the coherence of your papers, see if the first and last paragraphs have some obvious relations.

In most published writing, the first and last paragraphs of a book, a chapter in a book, or an article have such coherence that you can read them without reading the intervening material and have a fairly good idea of what comes between. Now and then you will find a piece of writing where the first and last paragraphs do not have a clear verbal connection. But writers wishing to be sure that their work holds together can help their efforts by seeing to it that each paper ends in a paragraph that reflects some words and thoughts appearing in the first.

Note the sample paper in Chapter 5. It begins with a reference to the online biography of Woodrow Wilson available on the Internet from the White House and comments on Woodrow Wilson's reputation as a great liberal statesman. It ends with another reference to that online biography, suggesting that it does not tell the whole story of Wilson's political legacy. Study other articles in published journals to see for yourself how often this principle is observed in the professional writing of history. Turn through the pages of *The American Historical Review,* seeing first and last paragraphs mirroring each other. (Looking at first and last paragraphs is also a good way to see if the article includes information you may want to use in your own work.) You can also see that this mirroring of first and last paragraphs appears in popular journals of opinion such as *The Atlantic* or *The New Yorker.*

4. Begin most sentences with the subject.

Sentences are statements about subjects. In published American English, about three-fourths to four-fifths of the sentences and independent clauses within sentences begin with the subject. This principle is often undermined by well-meaning writing teachers who tell students to vary sentences by inverting them—that is, by putting the verb before the subject. Or they tell students to begin with a participle or to do something else to keep the subject from coming first. Yet any examination of published English in widely read books and articles will show the proportion of openings with the subject that I have mentioned here. Most sentences that do not begin with the subject will begin with some sort of adverb—a word, a phrase, or a clause that fulfills the common adverbial function of telling when, where, how often, and how much. Now and then a sentence begins with a participle or a participial phrase. You will help keep your thinking clear if in writing sentences you think first of the subject, then of what you want to say about it. Our natural way of composing sentences, whether we speak or write, is to name a subject and then to make a statement about it. Sometimes inexperienced writers are paralyzed by the thought that they begin too many sentences with the subject. They feel a laudable desire to vary their sentences by changing the beginnings. Sometimes the result is obscurity.

This suggestion is more important than it may seem at first. Many sentences go astray and become hopelessly confused because writers don't know what they want to say. Be sure you write each sentence to make a clear statement about a subject. Don't bury your real subject in a dependent clause. Indeed, most readable writers use dependent clauses only once or twice in every three or four sentences. The main action of your sentence should be in the main clause. In that clause you should identify the subject as the element about which a statement is to be made.

5. Keep subjects as close to their verbs as possible.

The most readable writers seldom interrupt the natural flow of their sentences by placing a dependent clause after the subject. Like the general principle that most sentences begin with the subject, this is another one you can prove by reading almost any popular—and therefore readable—prose. It is not absolute. Every writer sometimes puts a word or a phrase or even a clause between a subject and a verb. But take care not to overdo it. Here is a fine, readable paragraph by historians Oscar and Lilian Handlin:

> The healing image meant much to a government, not all of whose statesmen were pure of heart and noble of impulse. On January 30, 1798, the House of Representatives being in session in Philadelphia, Mr. Rufus Griswold of Connecticut alluded to a story that Mr. Matthew Lyon of Vermont had been forced to wear a wooden sword for cowardice in the field. Thereupon Mr. Lyon spat in Mr. Griswold's face. Sometime later, Mr. Griswold went to Macalister's store on Chestnut Street and bought the biggest hickory stick available. He proceeded to the House, where, in the presence of the whole Congress and with Mr. Speaker urging him on, he beat Mr. Lyon about the head and shoulders. An effort to censure both actors in the drama failed.[5]

Note the close relation between subjects and verbs in this paragraph.

6. Use an occasional rhetorical question.

The rhetorical question is one that you, the writer, ask so you may define a problem you wish to pursue. You ask the question to answer it yourself. Here is a rhetorical question placed near the beginning of an essay on concepts of honor in the American South before the Civil War.

> Sometimes white men of the antebellum South pulled or tweaked one another's noses. Slaves never pulled anyone's nose; neither did white

---

[5]Oscar and Lilian Handlin, *Liberty in Expansion: 1760–1850* (New York: Harper & Row, 1989), 160.

women. Nose pulling was a meaningful act that appeared almost exclusively in the active "vocabulary" of white men. To pull a nose was to communicate a complex set of meanings to an antagonist and an audience. What did the act mean to the men who performed it and witnessed it?[6]

This rhetorical question opens to Professor Kenneth S. Greenberg ways of defining the concept of "honor" among Southern white men before the Civil War, and he has written a fascinating essay.

7. Use an occasional metaphor or simile to make a vivid statement.

Metaphors and similes appeal to some familiar experience or perception to illustrate something less familiar. Here is Civil War historian Shelby Foote, speaking of the danger sharpshooting snipers posed to troops in the line, even during lulls in the fighting:

> Because of them, rations and ammunition had to be lugged forward along shallow parallels that followed a roundabout zigzag course and wore a man down to feeling like some unholy cross between a pack mule and a snake.[7]

Such metaphors and similes enliven writing. Don't carry them to excess. Used discreetly, they can be a great help.

Avoid clichés, the tired old expressions that we have heard time and again. The essence of a cliché is its predictability. When we hear the beginning of the expression, we know what the end will be. We know that a bolt is always from the blue, although we seldom think that the person who speaks of the bolt from the blue is speaking of lightning striking on a clear day. We know that unpleasant facts are "cold, hard facts" and that the determining influence in a discussion is the "bottom line." These are expressions that require no thought on the part of the writer and that inspire no thoughts in the reader.

8. Avoid the passive voice whenever possible.

In sentences using the passive voice, the verb acts on the subject. In the active voice, the subject acts through the verb. Here is a sentence in the active voice: *President John F. Kennedy made the decision to invade*

---

[6]Kenneth S. Greenberg, "The Nose, the Lie, and the Duel in the Antebellum South," *The American Historical Review* (February 1990): 57.

[7]Shelby Foote, *The Civil War: A Narrative,* vol. 3 (New York: Random House, 1974), 297.

Cuba. Here is a sentence in the passive voice: *The decision was made to invade Cuba.*

You see at once a problem in the passive voice. It often hides the actor in the sentence. In the active voice we know who made the decision. In the passive voice we do not know who made the decision unless we add the somewhat clumsy prepositional phrase *by President John F. Kennedy.* Announcements by governments frequently use the passive voice. "Mistakes were made," says one government press release that I read not long ago. The passive shields us from knowing who made the mistakes.

Readable historians use the passive only when they have a reason for doing so. Use the passive when the obvious importance of the sentence is that the subject is acted upon: *Bill Clinton was elected to a second term as President of the United States in November 1996.* The passive may help keep the focus of a paragraph on a person or group where the agent is understood throughout. In the following paragraph from a history of the Russian Revolution of 1917 and afterward, the passive is used several times. Passive clauses are in italics. Study them to understand how the author uses the passive voice:

> The Kronstadt Naval Base, an island of sailor-militants in the Gulf of Finland just off Petrograd, was by far the most rebellious stronghold of this Bolshevik vanguard. The sailors were young trainees who had seen very little military activity during the war. They had spent the previous year cooped up on board their ships with their officers, who treated them with more than the usual sadistic brutality since the normal rules of naval discipline did not apply to trainees. Each ship was a tinderbox of hatred and violence. During the February Days the sailors mutinied with awesome ferocity. *Admiral Viren, the Base Commander, was hacked to death with bayonets, and dozens of other officers were murdered, lynched or imprisoned in the island dungeons. The old naval hierarchy was completely destroyed* and effective power passed to the Kronstadt Soviet. It was an October in February. *The authority of the Provisional Government was never really established, nor was military order restored.* Kerensky, the Minister of Justice, proved utterly powerless in his repeated efforts to gain jurisdiction over the imprisoned officers, *despite rumours in the bourgeois press that they had been brutally tortured.*[8]

[8]Orlando Figes, *A People's Tragedy: A History of the Russian Revolution* (New York: Viking, 1997), 394–395.

The focus of the paragraph is the consequence of the uprising of the sailors at Kronstadt. The passive helps to keep that focus.

The best rule is this: When you use the passive voice, ask yourself why you are doing it. If you do not have a clear reason for the passive, put your sentence in the active voice.

9. Keep sentences short enough to be manageable.

Sometimes writers lose control of their sentences and end with long, involved coils of words. Long sentences can be difficult. They slow readers down, hide your meaning, and make integration of that sentence to the sentences that come before it and after it difficult. Remember this cardinal rule: Every sentence in your essay picks up something from what has gone before and contributes something to what comes afterwards. To keep your own prose connected, you must observe this rule.

Always keep in mind the most important statement you want to make in every sentence. Don't entangle that statement with other information that you cannot develop or that is not a development of some previous information in your essay.

One way to keep sentences manageable is to avoid multiplying dependent clauses. Dependent clauses act as adjectives or adverbs and modify other elements in a sentence. They are necessary to writing. The most readable writing does not use a dependent clause in every sentence. A sentence may have one or two dependent clauses. But a couple of sentences that come after it may have no dependent clauses at all—like this paragraph from an article on the abnegation of French battlefield nurses in World War I. It is a dense but readable piece of prose:

> In the end the nurses' memoirs, like the commentaries, left intact the incongruity, even the opposition, of women and war. Targets of as much criticism as praise, nurses in their memoirs absolved themselves of the charge of pursuing feminine emancipation, solidarity, and values at the expense of masculine suffering by subordinating their wartime experience to the soldier's story. Rather than script a role for the volunteer nurse alongside the soldier in the War Myth, even the grimmest and most "realistic" of the nurses' memoirs placed the wounded soldier on a pedestal and the nurse, head bowed, at his feet, her emotional suffering a tribute to his sacrifice. In their personal accounts, France's nurse memoirists helped erase their own experiences from the public memory of the war. Their works did not reshape the War Myth to include

women; instead they commemorated World War I as the trench-fighters' war and confirmed the essence of the war experience as masculinity.[9]

My advice is not to avoid dependent clauses altogether, but to avoid making them so numerous that they make you lose control of your sentences and make your prose difficult to read. Don't write in the short, choppy sentences of a first-grade reader about Dick and Jane. But always ask yourself: Is this dependent clause necessary?

10. Don't overuse adjectives and adverbs.

Adjectives modify nouns; that is, they change the meaning of nouns somewhat. Adverbs modify verbs, adjectives, and other adverbs. Both adjectives and adverbs can weaken the words they modify. A good adjective or adverb well used in a necessary place can brighten a sentence. Too many of them thicken and slow down the flow of prose. The best advice is to use both sparingly.

The proportion of one adjective to every 12 or 13 words is fairly constant among published writers in America. The proportion of adverbs to other words is somewhat less. The proportion is not absolute. For some purposes you may have to use more adjectives and adverbs than normal. Be sure you need the adjectives and adverbs you use.

11. Write about the past in the past tense.

Inexperienced writers striving for dramatic effect will often shift into the historical present. They will write something like this:

> The issue as Calvin Coolidge sees it is this: The government has been intervening too much in private affairs. He is now the head of the government. He will do as little as possible. He takes long naps in the afternoon. He keeps silent when people ask him favors. He says things like this: "The chief business of the American people is business." He does not believe the government should intervene in the business process. Within a year after Coolidge leaves office, the Great Depression begins.

---

[9]Margaret H. Darrow, "French Volunteer Nursing and the Myth of War Experience in World War I," *The American Historical Review* (February 1996): 106.

The effort here is to provide life to the drama of history, to make it seem that it is all happening again as we read. But in American and British convention, we use the past tense to write about the past. The present becomes tedious after a while—and often confusing.

12. You may use the present tense in referring to the contents of writing.

It is permissible to use the present tense in describing a piece of writing or a work of art, because such works are assumed to be always present to the person who reads it or observes it. Therefore, you can say something like this: "The Fourteenth Amendment to the Constitution gives to the citizens of the various states all the rights guaranteed under the Federal Constitution."

Sometimes it may be better to use the past tense. This is especially true when you do not intend to give an extended summary of the work:

In his "Cross of Gold" speech delivered at the democratic National Convention in 1896, William Jennings Bryan took the side of the impoverished farmers who thought that inflation would help raise the prices they received for their crops.

CONCLUSION

If you think about the stylistic devices suggested in this chapter, you may begin looking more closely at writing you enjoy. Look at the forms writers use to keep you moving through their words. Learning to read is part of learning to write. You learn to read and write best not by consulting a book of grammar and syntax, but by noticing carefully the devices good writers use to woo readers.

8

Conventions

Historians are a broad community. Like most communities, they have their conventions, their ways of doing things. The conventions are not laws. People are not arrested and put in jail for violating them. Even so, members of the community notice when conventions are violated—just as they notice when someone blows his nose on a linen table napkin at a formal dinner or spits on the floor in church. Social conventions are violated if, when we are introduced to a perfect stranger, we howl with laughter and tell him that he is the ugliest person we have ever seen—even if he is. All conventions change from age to age and region to region. Even as they change, we depend on conventions and find them necessary. They help us know what to expect and have confidence in ourselves in various situations. They are not logical; they are simply customary. People once shook right hands when they met to prove they did not conceal a weapon in their fist. Left-handers, consequently, developed a sinister reputation in the ancient world because they could shake right hands and conceal a weapon in the left. I still put out my right hand, and so do the lefties I know, and we never think of weapons. Shaking hands is now merely a convention, and to refuse to shake hands with someone is an insult.

If anything, the conventions of writers are stricter than social conventions. If you violate the conventions, you run the risk of not being taken seriously. Your readers may even turn hostile because you seem to insult them by refusing to live up to their expectations. It makes no sense for a writer to irritate readers. It's hard enough to get them to pay attention to you without putting more obstacles in their way.

MANUSCRIPT CONVENTIONS

Most writers and most students nowadays use computers with word processing programs. Take advantage of the ability of the computer to generate clean copy. You can set the format of a computer to fit any manuscript style required by your teacher. You can mark up a printed copy of your work, then write the corrections onto your disc, and print out a clean copy. Computers make things easier for writers and readers alike.

The appearance of a manuscript tells readers many things about the writer. For one thing, they can tell what the writer thinks of them. A slovenly, scarcely legible manuscript is a sign that the writer cares little for the subject or the readers. The writer may care deeply—just as the parent who screams at children may love them. Still it is not pleasant for children to be screamed at, and it is not pleasant for readers to be forced to read an almost illegible paper.

The presentation of your paper calls to mind the presentation of food in an expensive restaurant. You would not tip a waiter who served the main course on a plate he snatched out of a pile of dirty dishes, wiped off with his sleeve, and banged down on the table in front of you before he filled it with a dipper from a bucket that had a mop in it. You would stalk out of the place in anger. Your hard-working teacher cannot stalk away from your sloppy paper. But if you violate the conventions, you may discover that the grade is less than you desire.

Formats vary. Your teacher may give you a format to follow. Lacking instructions, you will not go wrong if you follow the format of the model research paper in Chapter 5 of this book. Here are some generally accepted conventions.

1. Use 8½ × 11-inch white bond paper. Twenty-pound bond is best. It is heavy enough to handle easily and to make a nice contrast with the type or ink you use. Hard-pressed teachers reading three dozen research papers appreciate such favors. Do not turn in your final daft on flimsy colored paper.

2. Write on one side of the page only. Leave margins wide enough for comments your teacher may wish to make. Always double-space. Be sure the ink from the printer is dark enough to be read easily. Don't use a tacky, hard-to-read font. Use Times New Roman or Courier or some other clean, easy-to-read type font. If you submit a handwritten paper, use lined white paper and write in dark blue or black ink on every line. Do *not* use red, green, purple, or brown ink. Besides looking tacky, such inks tire your reader's eyes.

3. Use a cover page for your papers. On it place the title, your name, the name of your teacher, the name of your course, and the time your class meets. Teachers who grade many papers sometimes get

them mixed up on their desks. You will help your hard-working teacher immeasurably if you make it easy for him or her to place your work. The title page is not numbered, although it is counted as page 1, and the title itself should not be placed in quotation marks.

4. Number your pages. When you do not number pages, you make your paper difficult to comment on and almost impossible to discuss in class. Sometimes teachers copy papers to distribute to the class for discussion. Sometimes papers even fall on the floor, and pages are scattered. Numbering pages is one of the basic conventions of writing that have been around since we stopped using scrolls. Every word processing program numbers pages, usually in the menu for "layout" or "format." Don't be lazy. Find the steps your program uses to number pages, and number them. Be professional.

5. Fasten the pages of your paper with a paper clip or with a staple in the upper left-hand corner. Binders are a nuisance to the instructor, adding bulk and making it awkward to write comments in the margins. Don't use them.

6. Always make a second copy of your paper. Papers do get lost. Computers break down. We make mistakes on the keyboard and erase our work. Always make a second copy in case something happens to the original. If you use a computer, make a backup disc with your essay on it.

Corrections in the Final Copy

You should revise your paper enough to catch most casual errors—typos, misspellings, words left out, words duplicated, and so on. Even so, you may find other mistakes just as you are ready to hand in the paper. You may even want to revise slightly at the last minute. Carefully write these corrections in black ink. Be sure your changes are neat and legible.

USING QUOTATIONS

You will frequently quote both from primary and secondary sources. These quotations (not "quotes") will give authority to your papers. Here are some things to remember:

1. Use the American style for quotation marks. The primary American quotation mark is made with two apostrophes set together like this:

"History is the essence of innumerable biographies," Thomas Carlyle said.

2. Quotations within quotations are set off with single apostrophes like this:

Wilcox declared, "I entirely reject Carlyle's statement that 'History is the essence of innumerable biographies' because history is both more and less than biography."

3. Periods and commas used at the end of a quotation always go within the quotation marks:

"We learn from history that we learn nothing from history," Hegel said.

Voltaire said, "The history of the great events of this world is scarcely more than the history of crimes."

4. A comma, a colon, or a semicolon used before a quotation to introduce it is placed before the first quotation marks:

Thomas Jefferson said this: "Blest is that nation whose silent course of happiness furnishes nothing for history to say."

In worrying about predestination, Thomas Aquinas said, "Man has free choice, or otherwise counsels, exhortations, commands, prohibitions, rewards, and punishments would be in vain."

Mrs. Carter Harrison, wife of a former mayor of Chicago, denounced the film *Birth of a Nation* in unambiguous terms: "It is the most awful thing I have seen."

5. A question mark at the end of a quotation goes within the final quotation marks if the quotation itself is a question. It goes outside the final quotation marks if the quotation is not a question but is used within a question.

Question mark that is part of the quotation:

> Professor Young posed this question: "Why was a blatantly racist movie such as *Birth of a Nation* so popular?"

Question mark not part of the quotation:

> What did Francis Hackett, writing of the Reverend Thomas Dixon in the March 20, 1915, *New Republic,* mean when he said, "So far as I can judge from this film, as well as from my recollection of Mr. Dixon's books, his is the sort of disposition that foments a great deal of the trouble in civilization"?

6. Semicolons and colons always go outside the final quotation marks setting off a quotation:

> "He is yellow because he recklessly distorts Negro crimes, gives them a disproportionate place in life, and colors them dishonestly to inflame the ignorant and the credulous"; such was the judgment of Francis Hackett on the "yellow journalism" of the Reverend Thomas Dixon, author of the novel made into the movie *Birth of a Nation.*

7. It is nearly always better to use shorter quotations rather than longer ones. You can often incorporate a phrase or a clause from a source and give the flavor and the information you want to convey:

> Bruce Catton called the battle between the ironclad ships *Monitor* and *Merrimack* a "strange fight," for, as he said, "Neither ship could really hurt the other."

8. For any quotation longer than four or five lines, indent the entire quotation five spaces, and set it up as a block within your text. Double-space the block quotation, and do not enclose it with quotation marks. That is the advice of the *Chicago Manual of Style,* the bible of writers. Your teacher may want block quotations in single-space since your essays usually will not be for publication. Since it is difficult to edit single-spaced text, you should always double-space all material intended for publication.

DO NOT put quotation marks around a block quotation. Use quotation marks within the block quotation as they appear in the quoted source you are using.

9. Use ellipsis marks to indicate words you leave out between quotation marks with which you enclose quoted material. To make ellipsis marks, write three dots or periods, placing a space between each dot and whatever comes before and after it. Ellipsis marks . . . are made like this. Notice that there is a space between the word *marks* and the first dot that comes after it, a space between that dot and the next, and a space between the last dot and the word *are.* Here is an example. The original source is this:

> The Rosenbergs were not, prior to their arrest anyway, prominent national figures.

A quotation with some words left out indicated by ellipsis marks:

> In his history of political murder, Franklin L. Ford says of the Rosenbergs, executed for spying in 1953, "The Rosenbergs were not . . . prominent national figures."

DO NOT use ellipsis marks at the beginning of a quotation. Some writers have taken to beginning quotations with ellipsis marks to indicate that the quotation does not include all of a text. The quotation marks themselves indicate that the quoted material is separated from its source. Use of ellipsis marks at the beginning of a quotation is redundant and annoying. Do not do this: "Rebecca West says that the Archduke Franz Ferdinand of Austria-Hungary ". . . was a superb shot."

10. Change capital letters to lowercase or lowercase letters to capitals in quoted material when your purpose is to make the quotation fit into your own sentence. Here is a sentence from Richard Ellmann's biography *James Joyce* where Ellmann comments on the city of Trieste in 1920 when, in consequence of World War I, it had passed from Austrian to Italian rule:

> Under Austria the city had been full of ships; now the harbor was almost deserted.

Here is one way to use the quotation:

Ellmann, writing of Joyce's return to Trieste in 1920, says that "under Austria the city had been full of ships; now its harbor was almost deserted."

Do not use brackets to indicate that you have changed the capitalization of the *U* in *under*. The brackets are unnecessary and distracting.

OTHER CONVENTIONS ABOUT MECHANICS AND GRAMMAR

Most people feel anxious about grammar, supposing they do not know it well and imagining they make mistakes all the time. In fact, most of us know grammar well enough to use it reasonably well. Written language is more formal than spoken language; writing is more difficult than speaking. Sometimes in the physical labor of writing, our minds wander, and we make errors. That is, we violate conventions. Most people can spot their errors in grammar by reading their work carefully. You can usually trust your ear. When something doesn't sound right, check it out in an English handbook, or ask a friend. Writers collaborate all the time in real life; they should collaborate in school, too.

The grammar we use in writing is set by editors and writers themselves. It has not changed much in the last century. You encounter it in textbooks, magazines, daily newspapers, and your own writing. It is part of mass literacy—the general expectation in the modern world that most people can read. Mass production of any sort requires standardization and simplification of grammar. By following the standards, you increase the ease by which readers follow your work.

The following are sources of common difficulties. The list does not represent a complete summary of English grammar. If you have other problems, buy a good English handbook and study areas that give you the most difficulty.

1. Form the possessive correctly. The possessive shows ownership or a particular relation. We speak of *John's pen*, of *Prizzi's honor*, or *Charley's aunt*. Some writers and editors add only an apostrophe to singular nouns ending in *-s*. Thus we would have *Erasmus' works* or

Chambers' book. But the better practice is to make the possessive of these words as we do others. Thus it would be *Erasmus's works,* and *Chambers's book.*

For plural nouns that end in -*s*, add the apostrophe to form the possessive: *the Germans' plan; the neighbors' opinion.*

Plurals that do not end in -*s* form the possessive like singular nouns: *women's history; men's fashions; children's rights.*

2. Always make the plural of nouns ending in -*est* and -*ist* by adding -*s* to the singular form. The plural of *guest* is *guests;* the plural of *scientist* is *scientists;* the plural of *humanist* is *humanists.*

3. Be sure to note differences between plurals and collective nouns. For example, the singular is *peasant,* the plural is *peasants,* but the collective class in European history is called the *peasantry.* We may call a man or woman who works in a factory a *proletarian,* and a group of them on an assembly line might be called by Marxists *proletarians.* But Marx called the whole class the *proletariat.* We may speak of a *noble* or an *aristocrat* when we speak of highest social ranks in some societies, and a group of such people would be called *nobles* or *aristocrats,* but the whole class is called the *nobility* or the *aristocracy.*

4. Don't use an apostrophe to form a plural. Don't say, "The Wilsons' went to Washington." The correct form is *The Wilsons went to Washington.* The plurals of dates and acronyms do not use the apostrophe: We speak of the 1960s or the NCOs (noncommissioned officers such as sergeants) in the armed forces.

5. Make a distinction between *it's* and *its*. The contraction *it's* stands for *it is* or, sometimes, *it has.* The possessive pronoun *its* stands for "belonging to it":

> *It's* almost impossible to guarantee safe travel.

> *It's* been hard to measure the effects on the country.

> *The* idea had lost its power before 1900.

6. Use the objective case of pronouns correctly. The nominative or subjective case of pronouns includes the forms *I, we, he, she, who, they,* and *those.* The objective case includes forms such as *me, us, him, her, whom,* and *them.* The nominative case is used as the subject of a sentence or a clause:

I read Huizinga's books.

It was said that *he* was not the king's son.

The objective case should be used for the object of a preposition:

It was a matter between *him* and *me*.

Between *you* and *me,* I would say the policy was wrong.

The objective case should be used in an indirect object:

The President gave *her* a cabinet position.

The objective case should be used as the subject or an object of an infinitive. The infinitive is the verb form that includes the infinitive marker *to* and the dictionary form of the verb. Thus *to go, to be, to dwell,* and *to see* are all infinitives. The subject of the infinitive is a noun or pronoun that comes before the infinitive in a sentence, that does the action the infinitive expresses:

King Leopold wanted *him* to go at once to Africa.

In the preceding example, the person designated by the objective pronoun *him* will go to Africa. Since he will do the going, the action expressed in the infinitive *to go,* the pronoun *him* is the subject of the infinitive and is in the objective case.

The prime minister supposed both Russell and *me* to be damaged by the report.

In this example, the pronoun before the infinitive receives the action of the infinitive—here an infinitive phrase.

7. In clauses that begin with *who* or *whom, whoever* or *whomever*, the case of the pronoun is determined by how it is used in the clause, not how the clause is used in the sentence. Sometimes people eager to show that they know how to use *who* or *whom* will use *whom* where *who* is the correct choice. The problem is especially acute in the use of the word *whomever,* a variant of *whom.* They write sentences like this one: "In the nineteenth century, women and children worked for *whomever* paid them pennies for a 14-hour day." The fastidious writer of this sentence, knowing that the object of a preposition takes the objective case, writes the preposition *for* and puts *whomever* after it. But here the entire clause is the object of the preposition. The pronoun should be *whoever* because it is the subject of the clause. The pronoun is governed by how it is used in the clause, not by how the clause is used in the sentence. So the sentence should read: "In the nineteenth century, women and children worked for *whoever* paid them pennies for a 14-hour day."

The same principle applies in a common sentence form where a parenthetical clause appears after the pronoun *who*. You should **not** write this:

> The Indians *whom* Custer thought were only a small band in fact numbered in the thousands.

You **should** write this:

> The Indians *who* Custer thought were only a small band in fact numbered in the thousands.

The clause that determines the case of *who* is this: *who were only a small band.* The words *Custer thought* are parenthetical.

8. Use commas in the following instances:

a. Commas set off independent clauses from one another. Independent clauses can usually stand by themselves as sentences:

> The McNary-Haugen bill would have provided subsidies for American farmers, but President Coolidge vetoed it in 1927.

> Peru and Ecuador threatened to go to war over a border dispute, but they signed a treaty in 1941, ending the conflict.

> The people of the United States decided that they must give up Prohibition, for warfare among bootleggers was making the streets run with blood.

b. Use commas to set off long introductory phrases and clauses:

> Even after the transcontinental railroad was completed in 1867, some pioneers still made the trip West by covered wagon.

> After the American entry into the war of 1917, the victory of the Allied Powers over the Germans was assured.

c. Use commas to set off items in a series:

> President Franklin D. Roosevelt moved to solve problems of unemployment, banking, and despair.

> William Jennings Bryan campaigned for the presidency in
> 1896 by traveling 18,000 miles, making 600 speeches, and at-
> tacking the "monied interests."

d. Use commas to set off nonrestrictive clauses and phrases. You
can remove the nonrestrictive clause and still have an intelligible
sentence:

> Henry David Thoreau, *one of the greatest American writers,*
> died of tuberculosis.

Do not use commas to set off restrictive clauses—clauses necessary if the
main statement of the sentence is to be correctly understood:

> The man *who robbed the bank on one day* came back the next
> and stole all the calendars.

e. Commas separate two or more adjectives before a noun when
you can substitute the word *and* for the comma and still have a sensible
sentence:

> Ralph Waldo Emerson was a tall, frail, and elegant man.

[You could say, "Ralph Waldo Emerson was a tall and frail and elegant
man."] Do not use commas between adjectives where you cannot sensi-
bly replace the comma with *and.* You can say *The three old maple trees
stood on the hill,* but you cannot say, *The three and old and maple trees
stood on the hill.*

f. Be sure that clauses acting as adjectives clearly modify the
noun they are intended to modify in the sentence. Modification is usually
clearest when the modifying clause comes immediately after the noun it
modifies. Often confusions in modification result when a writer puts too
much in one sentence. Don't say this:

> Japanese bankers in the nineteenth century thought that learn-
> ing Chinese was necessary to doing business in the interior of
> China, which English bankers rejected.

In reading his sentence rapidly (as we read most things), we are suddenly
struck by confusion. What did English bankers reject? Doing business in
the interior of China? China itself? The interior of China? The sentence
needs to be recast:

> Japanese bankers in the nineteenth century thought that learn-
> ing Chinese was necessary to doing business in the interior of

> China, but British bankers thought the Chinese should learn English.

Sometimes the problem arises when writers follow the admirable policy of keeping subject and verb close together, but then decide to tack an adjectival clause on the end of the sentence, and so cause confusion:

> The Dreyfus Case weakened confidence in the French Army which unleashed furious passions in the French public.

The writer meant to say this:

> The Dreyfus Case unleashed furious passions in the French public and weakened confidence in the French army.

9. Make your subject and verb agree. Problems can arise when you have a prepositional phrase with a plural object after a single subject. Not this:

> His statement of grievances *were* read to the assembly.

But this:

> His statement of grievances *was* read to the assembly.

Use singular verbs after indefinite pronouns such as *anybody, everybody, anyone, everyone, somebody, someone, either, neither,* and *none*.

> Everyone *was* ready.

> Neither *was* possible.

None is occasionally used with a plural verb. Most writers still prefer to say, *None of the advantages **was** as important as the sum of the disadvantages.*

Some collective words give problems. More traditional writers still say, "The majority of her followers *was* not convinced." But some will say, "The majority of his followers *were*," seeing *majority* as a collective noun that can take a plural verb. The sky will not fall if you use either form.

The phrase *a number of* followed by a prepositional phrase with a plural noun always takes a plural verb: *A number of the spectators were more interested in the fight than in the football game.*

10. Be sure that participial phrases at the beginning of a sentence modify the grammatical subject.

> Betrayed by his trust of unscrupulous friends, Warren G. Harding died just in time to receive a respectful funeral.

You can make your prose incomprehensible and even ridiculous if you violate this rule:

> Living in a much less violent society, the idea that every man, woman, and child in the United States has a right to his or her very own assault rifle seems ridiculous to most Canadians.

Who or what lives in that less violent society? The idea? The sentence should read like this:

> Living in a much less violent society, Canadians find ridiculous the idea that every man, woman, and child in the United States has the right to his or her very own assault rifle.

Avoid making an opening participle modify an expletive *it*. The expletive *it* is the pronoun without a referent and used as a subject: *It will rain*. The *It* does not refer to a previous noun. Avoid constructions like this: "Steaming towards Europe, it seemed wise to him to hide from photographers on the ship." Instead say this: *Steaming towards Europe, he tried to avoid photographers on the ship.*

11. Don't break the parallel form of a series.

English and American writers often use words or phrases in a series, often in units of three. We speak of exorcising a demon in the Middle Ages "by bell, book, and candle." We write sentences like this: "The moral principle of seeking the greatest good for the greatest number motivated Rousseau, Bentham, and Mill." The units in the series must stand as grammatical equals. Therefore, you should not write sentences like this: "Richelieu wanted three things for France—authority for the king, an end to religious strife, and he also wanted secure 'natural' frontiers." The first two elements of this faulty series are nouns modified by prepositional phrases, but the last element is a clause. The sentence should be rewritten like this: *Richelieu wanted three things for France—authority for the king, an end to religious strife, and secure 'natural' frontiers.*

12. Do not join independent clauses with commas alone. Don't write this:

> The Fugitive Slave Act required free states to return escaped slaves to their owners in the South, in effect it removed the limits of safety for fleeing slaves from the Ohio River to the Canadian border.

You can put a period after the word *South* and begin a new sentence with *In effect,* or you can replace the comma with a semicolon and leave the sentence otherwise as it is.

13. Avoid confusion in making pronouns refer to antecedents.
Pronouns stand for nouns. Definite pronouns such as *he, she, it, him, her, they, them,* and *their* stand for nouns that usually appear somewhere before them in a sentence or paragraph. Be sure to make the pronoun reference clear even if you must revise the sentence considerably. Don't do this:

> The Czechs disdained the Slovaks because they were more cosmpolitan.

To whom does the pronoun *they* refer? Were the Czechs or the Slovaks more cosmopolitan? You must rewrite the sentence:

> The more cosmopolitan Czechs disdained the more rural Slovaks.

Appendix A

Book Reviews

Reviewing books is an essential part of the historian's profession. Reviewing books is also a good way to train yourself in understanding how the discipline of history works. Your teacher may ask you to write a review of an important book. Before you begin, look at journals that carry book reviews about the period and the region you are studying. Almost all journals in history carry book reviews, some of them long essays. An hour or two spent in the periodical room of your library reading reviews will help you understand the form and imitate it in your own review. If you find several scholarly reviews of the book you are reviewing yourself, you may learn a great deal about the book and its author, and you will also see issues you might choose to write about.

Remember! Fundamental honesty requires you to say so if you take something from a review that someone else has written of the book you are reviewing for your course.

Here are some pointers that will help you write good reviews.

1. Always give the author's major theme, his or her motive for writing the book. You will most often find that motive expressed in the preface, which you should always read. It is a good idea to read the preface, the introduction, and the last chapter of a book before you read the complete work. By reading the last chapter, you see where the author is heading as you read the rest of the book. One of my students once pounded the table and shouted "NO," when I said he should read the last chapter first. I told him history books are not novels, and he seemed mollified.

2. Summarize briefly the evidence the author presents.

3. Identify the author, but don't waste time on needless or extravagant claims about him or her. It is a cliché to say that the author is "well qualified" to write a book.

4. Avoid lengthy comments about the style of the book. It's fine to say that the style is good, bad, interesting, or tedious. If a book is especially well written or if it is incomprehensible, you may quote a sentence to illustrate a good or bad style, but don't belabor the point.

5. Avoid generalizations such as, "This book is interesting," or "This book is boring." If you do your job in the review, readers can tell whether you find it interesting or boring. And remember, if you are bored, the fault may be in you rather than the book. I still recall my Ancient History professor at the University of Tennessee who, when I said reading Plutarch bored me, declared sternly, "Mr. Marius, you have no right to be bored with Plutarch." He was right.

6. Avoid passionate attacks on the book. Scholarship is not always courteous, but it should be. Reviewers who launch savage attacks on books usually make fools of themselves. They may even win friends for the book they seek to demolish.

7. Don't feel compelled to say negative things about the book. If you find inaccuracies, say so, and if you disagree with the writer's interpretation here and there, say that, too, giving your reasons in a civil tone. Remember that petty complaints about the book may make you look foolish or unfair. Don't waste time pointing out typos unless they change the meaning the author intends.

8. Judge the book the author has written. You may wish the author had written a different book. You might write a different book yourself. But the author has written *this* book. If the book did not need to be written, if it adds nothing to our knowledge of the field, if it makes conclusions unwarranted by the evidence, say so. But don't review the book as if it should be another book.

9. Always remember that every good book has flaws. The author may make some minor errors in fact or some questionable judgments. Even so, the book may be extremely valuable. Don't condemn a book outright because you find some mistakes. Try to judge the book as a whole.

10. Try to bring something from your own experience—your reading, your thoughts, your reflections, your recollections—to the book. If you are reviewing a book about early twentieth-century China, and if you have traveled in China, you may bring your own impressions to the review of the book. Try to make use of a broad part of your education when you review a book. If you have read other books in other classes that are relevant to this class, say something about those books in your review. If you know facts the author has overlooked, say so.

11. Avoid writing as if you possess independent knowledge of the author's subject when in fact you have taken all you know from the book itself. Don't pretend to be an expert when you are not. Be honest.

12. Quote selectively but fairly from the book you are reviewing. Quotations give some sense of the tone of the book. They may express thoughts in a sharp and pungent way. The prose of the author you review may help spice up your own review.

13. Avoid long chunks of quotation. You must show your readers that you have absorbed the book you review. If you give them too many long quotations, they may suppose you are asking them to do the reflection and analysis you should have done yourself.

14. Read the book. That may be the most important advice about writing a book review. Now and then even professional historians don't read the books they review in journals. You can see their errors when outraged authors write to protest. Don't let that happen to you!

Appendix B

Essay Examinations

Essay examinations are not like the other kinds of papers that I have discussed in this book. Nevertheless, as the name "essay exam" insists, they are essays—essays to be done within a given time in circumstances where you must rely entirely on your memory, without the aid of notes or the reference room of a library. Essay exams test what you know and how you think about what you know. They are to some degree artificial creations; historians do not write under the strictures of the standard essay exam format. They write and revise, go back to their sources, and revise some more.

Such exams are, however, perhaps the most comprehensive test of how much you have learned in an academic course, and they are so much a part of the Western academic scene that you doubtless already have much experience with them. The best examinations allow you to show your knowledge about the facts and some sources for these facts and to prove that you can make judgments about them.

The best way to prepare for an essay exam is to attend class diligently and take good notes. I've already said that the best way to take notes is to jot down words and phrases, not to try to take down everything your professor says. As soon as you can after class, sit down at your computer or your yellow pad, and using these scratch notes as your foundation, write out an account of what the professor has said. Notice in particular those things that he or she emphasizes, those things that he or she repeats again and again. When something is unclear, ask someone else in the class what the point was. Use reference books, including your textbooks, encyclopedia, dictionaries, to look up names that may be somewhat confusing to you.

All this takes time, of course, and college students are busy, many of them working at jobs to support themselves in school. It is hard to take the time to go over notes immediately after taking them, and it's time-consuming to write them out after you have come from the class. Yet if you force yourself to take the time, you will discover that you may save time in the long run. You will impress the data on your brain as you write out your notes about it. You will become acquainted with your own notes, and when the exam draws near, you can face it without cramming for it ahead of time because you will already know most of the material. It's a good idea to get together with friends and to come up with a collection of class notes that you have all cooperated in putting together. I observe students who get together and talk about the class by themselves; they are both more interesting in class and more likely to make the highest grades when testing time rolls around.

Another good tactic in preparing for an essay exam is to think what questions you would ask if you were the professor. Pay attention to what the professor emphasizes in class and try to write questions that would take that emphasis into account. A professor who gives detailed lectures on why the South lost the Civil War is very likely to ask you that question on an exam. Professors have a sporting instinct that students should recognize, for professors feel that if they have spent a good long time discussing a subject in class, it's only fair to expect students to know something about it. If you write out questions of your own, you will be surprised at how well you sometimes can read your professor's mind.

Once you have the examination, follow the directions carefully. *Read the questions.* I've been surprised all my life at how often students will read the question carelessly and write an essay having almost nothing to do with the topic being examined.

Judge how much time you can spend on each question. Don't spend all your time writing on one question so that you either don't answer the other questions at all or else do so in such a skimpy fashion that you don't answer them well. After college you will discover that allocating time is one of the most essential tasks of a human being, and writing a good exam is good training for what will come later on.

In looking at the questions, determine what kind of writing each of them calls for. Your primary task may be to tell a story, to narrate: "Trace the career of Martin Luther from the Indulgence Controversy of 1517 to his appearance before the Diet of Worms in 1521." You will tell a sequence of events from 1517 to 1521, being careful to choose the most important steps in this part of Luther's career. Your professor will judge you on how well you tell the story, your sense of what was important and what was less important, and the facility with which you grasp the essence of the story.

Often you will be asked to explain the historical significance of an event, a document, or a person. "Significance" in history means that the topic of the question accounts for some change, some development, some influence in what came afterwards. You might get a question like this on an exam in modern Chinese history: "Discuss the significance of the heroic image of Sunyatsen in the developing ideologies of Chinese Communism and its 'Nationalist' opponents." To answer this question you must first define the "heroic image" of Sunyatsen as he became the leader in the effort to free the Chinese from European imperialist control. Why did he become a hero? Then you must tell what his program for China included. And then you must summarize briefly the different ways the Communists under Mao Zedong and the rival Kuomintang party under Chang Kaishek took over his message for their own ends. Always when you answer a question about significance, you must try to consider what might have happened in the absence of the significant event. If Sunyatsen had not lived, what might have happened in China? Would the various revolutions China experienced in the twentieth century have taken on a different character?

So here are the steps in answering a question about significance. Define the significant person, text, or event. Show how the influence of the significant event developed, taking care to mention that this influence may have taken several different forms among different groups. If possible try to weigh what might not have happened in the absence of the person, text, or event. You cannot be absolute about suggesting what might have happened but did not. Such matters lie beyond the powers of mere historians and belong properly to soothsayers, magicians, and astrologers. So don't pretend that you are certain of what would have happened in the absence of this or that in history. But you can see what did happen, and you can make some plausible conjectures about what might have happened had other circumstances prevailed.

Related to questions about significance are short questions that ask you to identify various historical persons, events, or documents. Your professor may ask these questions to see if you command a broad area of material covered in the course. You are not expected to spend much time on such questions, but you are expected to answer the journalistic questions about the item—tell who was involved, what he or she did or what happened, when, where, and why the document, person, or event is important.

History professors love comparison questions because such questions force you to integrate at least two parts of the course. In effect, the professor gets two answers from you for the price of one question, and you are required to demonstrate the flexibility of your mind and the quantity of your knowledge about the works: for example, "Compare Thomas More's *Utopia* and Machiavelli's *The Prince*, both written in 1516."

A comparison question assumes that you will find similarities and differences in the two works. You should focus on the important places where comparisons can be made. You could say that in their respective works, More and Machiavelli were both preoccupied with reform. There were differences in what kind of reform they wanted. More's reform was to make society more virtuous and rational. Machiavelli wanted reform in the Italian state system so Italians could rule themselves, free of the "barbarians" from France and Germany whose armies swept down into Italy whenever they wanted. Both More and Machiavelli believed in the fundamental selfishness of human nature, and so their efforts at reform had to take this lack of virtue into account. More's Utopians banded together to destroy private life so that individualism, the greatest threat to virtue in More's view, might be suppressed in collective government in a republican society run by fathers. Machiavelli believed national unity might come under a prince who understood how to manipulate people and by various theatrical acts might lead them to unity.

We need not go on in these details, but the method of comparison should be obvious. You should show similarities, recognizing that in different people or works or events the similarities quickly branch off into differences. You should follow these differences in their most important branches, perhaps concluding with some words on the similar motivations and perhaps the similar successes or failures of both. Comparison questions, and indeed the very act of comparison, help work against the temptation to make everybody in one period of history seem the same. Far too often people speak of "the Renaissance view of humankind" or "the Medieval mind" as if everyone were agreed about fundamental issues in the Renaissance or the Middle Ages. That notion is one of the biggest of historical fallacies. To compare, for example, Machiavelli and More is to see how radically different two people living at the same time can be.

You may be asked to analyze an important text as part of an exam. Perhaps your professor may give you a paragraph from an important historical document and ask you to tell what it means. (This is one of my own favorite exam questions.) Very likely your professor will have lectured on this document at length during the course. Your task will be to look carefully at the document to see exactly what it says, pondering at the same time exactly what it does not say. Any important document has layers of meaning, and the modern temper is not to take for granted any simple understanding of a text. One of the insights offered us by the literary theorists called deconstructionists is that almost any text contains some contradictions, either explicit or implied. In American history one of the best known of these contradictions lies in our Declaration of Independence where we are solemnly assured, "We hold these truths to be self-evident, that all men are endowed by their Creator with certain unalienable rights, that among these are life, liberty, and the pursuit of happiness, and that to secure these rights, governments are instituted among men . . . ." Yet at the moment this declaration was penned and heroically signed, many of its adherents—including Thomas Jefferson who wrote most of it—held African slaves in bondage, men, women, and children who had no liberty, who had little opportunity to pursue happiness, and whose lives were dictated by owners over whom the slaves had no control. Yet the Declaration of Independence provides no hint of slavery.

So when we analyze a document, we look closely at the words, and we listen carefully for the silences. We can then see in the document a window opening onto the times, and we understand history better.

Some exam questions will ask you to argue a point. These essays are difficult and challenging. As in writing any kind of argument, the point on an argument in an exam question is not to prove one side or another beyond any doubt. I hope you know by now that historians seldom prove anything beyond any doubt. You cannot resolve all doubts and eliminate all contrary opinions in the few minutes you have on an examination. You can, however, show that you know the material and that you can think about it intelligently and that you can make a plausible case for what it means. As always in an argument, you should show some familiarity with arguments contrary to your own and provide a few words about why you reject them.

In responding to any exam question, you must be specific. You must name people, dates, documents, places—answering the journalistic questions that I have pounded on throughout this little book. Who? What? Where? When? Why? These questions should haunt your mind, and you should always be trying to answer them as you read and write. Exams may seem threatening. But if you have prepared for them, spent time on them, thought about them beforehand, you may discover that they offer you an opportunity to shape your knowledge, integrate various parts of it, and produce something that may be not only a source of pleasure but also of pride.

Credits

Index